In *What If They Knew? Secrets of an Impressive Woman,* Lisa Payne helps us shine light on our greatest fears, as she empowers us to embrace the darkest, most hidden aspects of ourselves—the secrets we may not even know we've been keeping.

Embrace this book with the same open-mindedness that I did and you, too, will find yourself letting go of the "should've beens" and "could've beens," while learning how to love yourself right now . . . as you are!

Crystal Andrus
Founder of The SWAT Institute
(Simply Woman Accredited Trainer)
Bestselling Author and International Speaker

What If They Knew?

Secrets of an Impressive Woman

LISA L. PAYNE

BALBOA.
PRESS

A DIVISION OF HAY HOUSE

ISBN: 978-1-4525-4718-3 (sc)
ISBN: 978-1-4525-4717-6 (e)
ISBN: 978-1-4525-5030-5 (hc)
Library of Congress Control Number: 2012902562

Balboa Press books may be ordered through booksellers or by contacting:

Balboa Press
A Division of Hay House
1663 Liberty Drive
Bloomington, IN 47403
www.balboapress.com
1-(877) 407-4847

Because of the dynamic nature of the Internet, any web addresses or
links contained in this book may have changed since publication and
may no longer be valid. The views expressed in this work are solely those
of the author and do not necessarily reflect the views of the publisher,
and the publisher hereby disclaims any responsibility for them.

The author of this book does not dispense medical advice or prescribe the use
of any technique as a form of treatment for physical, emotional, or medical
problems without the advice of a physician, either directly or indirectly. The
intent of the author is only to offer information of a general nature to help
you in your quest for emotional and spiritual well-being. In the event you use
any of the information in this book for yourself, which is your constitutional
right, the author and the publisher assume no responsibility for your actions.

Any people depicted in stock imagery provided by Thinkstock are
models, and such images are being used for illustrative purposes only.
Certain stock imagery © Thinkstock.

Printed in the United States of America
Balboa Press rev. date: 6/13/2012

Also by the Author

Lisa L. Payne is a contributing author of *Freeing Godiva: A Woman's Journey of Self-Empowerment* by Insight Publishing, 2012

Dedicated to the most Impressive Woman
In my Life
My Mother
Bernice Payne

Reclaiming the parts of ourselves that we have relegated to the shadow is the most reliable path to actualizing all of our human potential. – Debbie Ford

Contents

Part One

Part Two

Acknowledgments

To the staff at Balboa Press. Thank you for your support, encouragement, and diligence. Thank you for keeping me on task and being the beacon of light at times when I felt lost in the words. Thank you for welcoming me into your community of authors. It has been a privilege to work with you.

To my parents. You were my first teachers. Always there for me, your support has been immeasurable. You are shining examples of integrity, balance and contribution. I thank you from the bottom of my heart.

To my children. Since you came into my life, you have provided me with daily inspiration to be the best that I can be. It is an incredible privilege to be your mother, to watch you grow and develop into extraordinary people. I feel truly blessed for your support and understanding. You are both wise beyond your years and have taught me many valuable lessons. My Sunshine and my Moonlight, I love you.

To Crystal Andrus. For the contribution you are in the world, thank you. For encouraging me let go of my limiting beliefs, take a leap of faith, and shine my light, I am grateful. For believing in my message and sharing your own insight with my readers in the foreword, I am deeply touched. It is an honour to know you.

To my love. You have provided me with a safe place to express myself fully. This is the most wonderful gift. Thank you for loving me. Thank you for allowing me to love you back.

To my friends. You have blessed me with your presence in my life. I am grateful for the love and support you have shown me and my children. Thank you for being part of my village.

To all the Impressive Women in my life. There are too many to name and so much to say that words can hardly express what you mean to me. You inspire me to greatness in everything I do. It is for you that this book has been written.

Foreword

CRYSTAL ANDRUS

What if you discovered that you've been wasting unlimited amounts of precious energy, beauty, passion, and success trying to "cover up" who you'd never want anyone to think you are?

What if you discovered that the things you most resist and reject about yourself—the shame, guilt, embarrassment, and denial—are merely unacceptable and intolerable beliefs you've been taught; fears that are robbing you of your joy, hope, excitement, and love?

What if you discovered the truth: Secrets make us sick—physically, emotionally, mentally, financially, and spiritually.

In *What If They Knew? Secrets of an Impressive Woman*, Lisa Payne helps us shine light on our greatest fears, as she empowers us to embrace the darkest, most hidden aspects of ourselves—the secrets we may not even know we've been keeping.

Denial is an amazing thing. It blocks us from seeing ourselves... *seeing the truth*... through accurate lenses. Denial keeps us trapped in our story.

Throughout the pages of this book, you'll read confessions from different women—women just like you and me. Once you are finished, I encourage you to ask yourself which women (which stories) you find to be the most intolerable, unacceptable, or inappropriate.

Here you will find your truth...

Your own distaste will shine light on your denial and greatest fears: The women you love the most are most like you, and the women you dislike the most are most like you!

Throughout my life, I (like many of the women you will soon read about) had many secrets and shameful stories. I convinced myself if I could just "do enough, I'd be enough."

But it wasn't until I finally stopped running, fixing, helping, caretaking, rescuing, buying, giving, doing, hiding, and denying that I was able to heal my own wounded little girl, make peace with her past, set stronger boundaries, and most importantly, begin forgiving myself for what I did or didn't do right.

I realized I couldn't like some parts of me, while rejecting the rest of myself. I had to learn to love me... in spite of me.

I had to learn to forgive.

I had to let go of my shame, guilt, fear, and blame.

I had to surrender my need to please, impress, and outdo everyone... *especially myself.*

I had to learn to love my fat, my faults, my mania, my depression, my wrinkles, and my mistakes, so that I could stop exerting so much energy into hiding them.

It was time to shine light on all my great qualities, without being afraid someone would discover my bad ones.

It was time I got on the right path for me. It was time I started listening to myself. It was time I started loving myself!

Living with self love isn't about forgetting about those you love. It isn't about having "abs of steel," a monstrous bank account, or hundreds of friends and admirers [although these things might happen once you do love yourself].

Self love is about living in alignment with who you really are: A divine, special, holy child of God—pure, innocent, passionate, trusting, loving, forgiving, courageous, and fearless... *and certainly, not perfect!* [And yet, it is our imperfections that do indeed make us so loveable.]

Self-love is not a noun... it's a verb. It's a journey that never ends. It is a daily way of living, loving, speaking, eating, moving, giving, and receiving.

Self-love is a far cry from selfish narcissism. In fact, it is the only thing that will ever bring you lasting happiness.

Embrace this book with the same open-mindedness that I did and you, too, will find yourself letting go of the "should've beens" and "could've beens," while learning how to love yourself right now... as you are!

Great job, Lisa! Bravo to you!

Warmly,

Crystal Andrus
Founder of The SWAT Institute
(Simply Woman Accredited Trainer)
Bestselling Author and International Speaker

Introduction

The Impressive Woman. You know her. You admire her. Maybe you envy her or love to hate her (for shame).

This is what she looks like:

She's got it all together. She impresses people wherever she goes—work, school, home, playground, fundraisers, bottle drives, beach fires, and family reunions. She is caring, intelligent, and fun. She bakes delicious chocolate-chip cookies, looks as great in jeans as she does in a dress, and always has time for a friend in need. She has frailties but hides them well. She doesn't dwell on them, but she has fears and limiting beliefs, too.

She looks like your mother, your sister, your girlfriend, your colleague, your boss. She is all of us. She is you. She is me.

Life has been quite good to me over the years. I consider myself an Impressive Woman for all that I am and all that I have done. I have been working on my self-awareness for the past ten years and, along my journey, have made tremendous progress. My life today barely resembles the life I led a decade ago. I have been deliberate in my choices and I have created a new reality that reflects my core values. I began my own business as a life coach and speaker, sharing my lessons learned with other people, with a mission of helping them define and execute their own vision of success. I deliver seminars, keynotes, and coaching programs. I have written articles and most recently, was the only Canadian to be featured in Insight Publishing's anthology, *Freeing Godiva: A Woman's Journey of Self-Empowerment.*

I have also had my share of troubles. I don't dwell on them much, trying my best to remain positive in the face of change and challenge. I have discovered, however, through much self-exploration and with the help of a couple of counsellors and coaches, that suppressing my worries, fears and doubts, has lead me to experience a number of health concerns that I haven't been able to shake. I have held the intention for a number of years to put my health first when it comes to creating success, but my commitment has not been as strong as I need to make progress. I have been putting bandages on my wounds, but that's not doing the trick; long-term healing is what I am really seeking. I know I deserve that, too, but I haven't been able to "make it happen". In December 2011, I finally *surrendered* [so hard!] and decided that my best course of action was to look inward. I was rewarded.

The idea for this book came from a meditation. For a few years now, I have been finding peace this way, usually a guided relaxation process where I clear my mind and listen to a soothing voice on a CD while lying in bed. This time was different. This meditation was long—45 minutes—and it was not guided. It was just me, and three other group participants, in the silence. We were asked by the leader to set an intention at the start; as I closed my eyes, I asked, "What do I need to do to heal my heart?" *I don't even know where that question came from* but once I released it, the answer was revealed.

First it was the cover of the book and the title, as clear and brilliant as could be. Then, one by one, the chapter titles rolled out and the layout. I wanted to stop the meditation and write everything down but I trusted that I would remember all that I needed, and I did. Within one hour following the meditation, I had the entire outline of the book mapped out in a journal. It flowed so effortlessly. It was amazing!

The meditation confirmed for me that *I have a voice*. I have been given a gift and it is my purpose to share with others so they may heal, too. We are all one. I am not alone in what I have experienced.

What If They Knew? uncovers the secrets of Impressive Women, with a chapter devoted to each woman's story. There is no need to read them in order. Each one stands on its own merits and you may find yourself reading certain ones because they strike a chord in you, even if you can't explain it. While they have all been penned by me, this book is not completely autobiographical. It was helpful for me to rely on some techniques taught by Debbie Ford in her book, *The Dark Side of the Light Chasers* [Penguin Group, New York, 2010], in order to connect with the shadow aspects of my personality. As I wrote, I found myself thinking about other women whose stories I have heard over the years and I felt responsible to include them as well. Many women represented here (all pseudonyms) have attended my workshops, confessed over coffee, whined over wine, and shared in the schoolyard. The similarities in our secrets are undeniable and, I believe, they make for a compelling book.

I invite you to read the confessions of these Impressive Women as they reveal their darkness, in Part One, and share their light in Part Two. They are women, just like you and me, who have found the courage to love themselves as they are, and let go of the fear that plagues us: *What if they knew? What would they think of us? Would they still love us? Would they still respect us?*

You will be captivated by the raw truth and emotion as they shed years of pent up anguish and fear and step into their authentic power. As they are released from bondage, you, the witness, will also be. YOU are an Impressive Woman whose time has come.

Yours in possibility,

Lisa L. Payne
Newfoundland & Labrador
Canada
March 2012

Part One

I am a Liar

For as a long as I can remember, I've been telling lies. It started out small. For instance, when I'm asked how I am, sometimes I reply, "I'm fine." But I'm really not. I have wondered why I don't just tell the truth. I keep thinking, *"What if they knew? What would they think of me? Would they love me less?"*

The lying started at a very young age. I was just trying to be the best little girl I could. I figured out very early on that my parents would like a good girl much more than a bad girl and so I fashioned my entire life around pleasing them... even if it meant telling lies. The thing is: once you start telling lies, it is much easier to keep going than to confess and speak the truth. Oh, what a tangled web we weave... and, don't I know it. Soon, the lies become your reality. You don't actually remember the truth. Oftentimes, the lies are more exciting and they create a persona that you like more than the real, boring you; also, it gets you what you want.

I have been rewarded for telling lies. I have gained a reputation for being an Impressive Woman, but it isn't true. As a child I was touted as the most agreeable, the most obedient, the most dependable. I became the child that everyone wanted to care for. Babysitters, camp counsellors and teachers all chose me as their pet. Of course, just when I would become subject to ridicule for being 'the chosen one', I would quickly spin a story to win the favour of my schoolmates and friends so that they would think I was just like them–*another lie.*

As an adult entering the workforce, I lied about my abilities. I took on projects for which I was not qualified and I put on the

1

face of the ultimate success story. In reality, I was fabricating a life that had no meaning to me. I towed the company line so I could win the favour of my bosses, at the expense of my own integrity and self-esteem. I have never felt worthy of the praise that I received, even when it was clear—in black and white—that I had achieved particular goals. I didn't feel worthy because a lifetime of lying had left me feeling like the real me couldn't possibly be good enough.

When I married, I thought that I was marrying a man who could accept me for who I really was and that the lying could finally stop. I later realized, however, the person he fell in love with was a complete shell of a person who chose her masks carefully, never fully revealing herself for fear of rejection. I created a life where each decision was made to elicit the outcome I desired. What everyone else (including my husband) saw as the 'perfect marriage' was actually make-believe. As I became the master manipulator, my inner struggles eventually got the best of me.

Throughout that relationship, as I became more and more aware of the truth of what I had become, I started to allow the buried aspects of me to come out. That resulted in what I had tried to avoid my whole life: conflict, disappointment, and hurt. As I began to release the true aspects of myself, along with my own self-loathing, the relationship began to crumble. I had to take responsibility. It was my fault.

What if they knew that I am a liar?

I am a Cheat

The first time I cheated was in grade two. I remember distinctly being asked to make a Christmas ornament of my own design and present it to the class. I was panicked. I was not a child who could make something from nothing... not the type who could draw for hours on end with blank sheets of paper. Don't get me wrong; I loved to color and do art projects, but my favourite activities were tracing other people's drawings and coloring. I liked to add my own color but I didn't feel quite capable of designing the concept out of thin air. So I copied.

With this particular creative assignment, I was afraid that I would be found out. I was afraid that everyone would discover that I really wasn't that good at art. As my lack of confidence in my own 7-year old artistic talent outweighed my sense of integrity, I found the best solution possible. My mother subscribed to a magazine for parents. In the December issue, there were numerous ideas for Easy Christmas Crafts for Children and I dove in like a scientist in search of a cure. My diligence was rewarded with the most perfect, but quite elaborate activity. I told Mom I needed to find a number of craft supplies for an art project at school and she obligingly took me shopping to get everything I needed. An artist herself, I believed that she was very impressed with my ambition and encouraged me to work hard on my "original" art piece. As I slaved away in my bedroom for hours that evening, she had no idea that I was doing my best to follow the pictures in the magazine—all in an effort to meet her exalted expectations.

Considering that I could not decipher all the instructions (I was only 7, remember), I managed to produce a very good facsimile of the craft and I proudly went to school the next day. The sense of pride I felt quickly turned to shame when I went to the front of the class. With my stomach in knots and my face as red as a beet, I passed my piece of artwork around the class to be admired by all. And admire it, they did. The teacher was very impressed at the level of detail that went into the construction and she awarded me first prize: a giant candy cane. The peppermint helped to settle my stomach somewhat and, thanks to the accolades, the great secret got bottled up inside me for many, many years.

This aspect of my personality surfaced a few more times throughout my life and often surrounded independent school work. I wrote the part of the periodic table that I couldn't remember on my arm, under my sweatshirt, on the day of my chemistry exam in high school. I got an advanced copy of questions to an economics quiz in university. And, once, when I had to present to a staff meeting, I used an article in *Canadian Business* to deliver some 'new' concepts in customer service that we may consider. The gnawing fear that someone would discover my secret has never been far from my mind.

What if they knew I am a cheat?

I am a Thief

Have you ever taken a peek in the medicine cabinet when you were at someone else's house? When you've had to crash at a friend of a friend's because you had too many glasses of wine at a birthday party, did you ever snoop through the bureau or nightstand to see what treasures lay within? I have done both but I admit to taking things a little bit farther... quite literally... I have taken things home!

Yes, since I was a young child I have been carrying guilt with me because I have lifted items from homes, stores, churches, and schools. Trinkets and items that would not likely be noticed are my preference. This isn't premeditated, folks, and I certainly don't take anything that is of much monetary value. Oftentimes, the target is one of a multiple item so I feel that the risk of it being noticed is even smaller. I'm not proud; in fact, I am ashamed at my behaviour.

Here is a sampling of things that I have stolen over the past 40 years:

- Pretty Christmas tree ornaments, from the back of the tree
- Socks, not always matching
- New toothbrush, still in the package
- Barrettes, especially sparkly ones
- Pens, fine point
- Sticky note pads, with company logos
- Fancy gift bags that look like they cost more than $1
- Empty picture frames

- Stuffed toys, neglected by the owners (this is really a rescue mission)
- Mood rings
- Cigarettes, singles from a pack already half smoked
- Condoms, (again) from a pack already being used
- Lipstick, the perfect shade only
- Gloves, the kind I've always wanted
- Frisbees, red ones only
- Gum, cinnamon

It doesn't make me feel good to know that I am taking things from other people but I do always consider that I will be nicer to the chosen items that the previous owner. I will appreciate them more. I will be more attentive and caring. And I do take the smallest amount of pleasure in the fact that I have never been caught. Who would ever suspect an Impressive Woman like me?

What if they knew I am a thief?

I am a Gossip

Is there anything more liberating then sitting around with a bunch of other women and sharing all the nasty things you heard about the one who is not there? Well, I guess, it may not be all that liberating... but it is fun! And I love to gossip. It is one of my secret passions. In fact, I rarely do it in groups because then everyone would think I was a gossip and that's not good for my Impressive Woman image. No, I prefer the one-on-one gossip, at a coffee shop, on a Sunday afternoon.

"Did you hear what so-and-so did on Friday night? Do you know who she's sleeping with now? Did you see what she wore to the gallery opening?" Great conversation starters, indeed! The juicier, the better. Sometimes, of course, the people that you know aren't nearly as exciting as those you wish you knew. That's when the conversation gets even better as my girlfriends and I speculate over who is doing what on Friday night, with whom they are sleeping, and what they wore wherever they went.

Gossip can really take on a life of its own and when you throw some wine in the mix, the sky is the limit to what stories can evolve. Usually, I admit, there are a few favourite topics. It's no different than how the tabloids focus on the same stars for weeks or years on end. These people are easy targets. Every day they do, say or wear things that simply elicit raised eyebrows, snickers, and blatant insults. It's like they asking for it, and we are just giving them want they want.

I have one acquaintance who supplies ample fodder for conversations and ensuing ridicule. The poor woman is nice enough but, *Jeez Louise*, does she really have to dress like a hooker and then complain about all the men who are constantly badgering her with gifts, dinners out, and hot, steamy, no-strings-attached sex?? Every now and then, I wonder if the reason we talk about her so much is that we would like a bit of that action!! Of course, not. We are the Impressive Women who know exactly what to do, say and wear at any given occasion; always appropriate, and never subjecting ourselves to the scrutiny of others.

I have never considered, until now, that people *could* be gossiping about me. That is kind of alarming! Imagine my life under a microscope. I don't think I could handle it. They could be talking about what I did last weekend. They could be talking about my choice of men, or God forbid, the long string of coffee dates that have never amounted to anything more. They could be talking about that dress I bought... I wonder if they think I'm too old to wear it with boots. This is too much... they can't be talking about me. That just wouldn't be fair!

What if they knew I am a gossip?

I am a Judge

I am a strongly opinionated woman. This may come from my upbringing where discussions around the dinner table were encouraged and often heated. If you had something to say, you had better be prepared for a debate. If you couldn't back up your argument with facts, you had better keep your mouth shut.

Perhaps, for this reason, I have always attracted people who are quite opinionated as well. I did, however, become uncomfortable when one of my ex-boyfriends displayed signs of being prejudiced. Was that ever unattractive! As I stated, I grew up around expressive individuals who didn't hold back what they thought about subjects like politics, religion, education, and social issues, but we always kept it pretty clean. No hitting below the belt. No singling out of races, creeds, genders. So when my wise friend told me that the offending boyfriend was just a reflection of my shadow self, I looked into this further and realized that I am a judge and I have been hiding from this reality because it isn't pretty and doesn't match my persona of an Impressive Woman.

When I got up close and personal with my inner judge, I found that she was ever-present—a barometer of sorts—that would be triggered whenever I saw something that didn't jive with my definition of good or proper. I am sad to say, if you are in my life in any way, I have judged you. Now, I probably haven't said anything out loud to you, or if I did, it was covered up in some kind of constructive criticism and you likely received it well. That's how I roll.

It turns out that I have been judging people, positively and negatively, for as long as I can remember. That's how I figured out what was right and wrong. From the moment I wake up, I put on my judge hat and navigate the day, praying for more right than wrong.

- "The coffee is too strong this morning."
- "Your hair looks lovely, honey."
- "Hey buddy, do you know *why* your car has an indicator?"
- "Ah, fresh flowers delivered to my office. *Somebody* loves me."
- "You're telling me the project is running late *and* over budget?"
- "Do you think you should have studied more?"
- "What do you mean 'you have to work late'?"
- "Can't *anyone* do anything right around here?"
- "Oh, you brought *merlot*."

The assessments and comparisons never stop. Honestly, when I think about it, it can be quite exhausting! But I own it. It is part of me. Like it or lump it.

The ownership of the title, Judge Jillian, came with much trepidation. After all, it was the trait that I hated the most in other people, especially boyfriends. It was a hard pill to swallow to admit to myself that I carry these same tendencies, even if I am more covert about my opinions. And, even more to the point, I certainly hope no one is judging me!

Really, there is no need. Clearly, not because I am perfect but because the person I judge most harshly is me. From morning to night, I must look at myself in the mirror one hundred times, adjusting and smoothing, sucking things in, examining every nook and cranny... and, sadly, there is always something to improve! I could have a full time job judging myself but I do like to take a break now and then; that's why it's good to have a wide circle of work colleagues, friends, acquaintances and strangers over whom I can look down and cast judgment.

What if they knew I am a judge?

I am a Slut

I thought about writing: *I am promiscuous*, but it feels like I am trying to cover up the facts with a fancier title. Ultimately, what I'm trying to say is that I like sex, I like having it with different people, and I like using sex to get what I want from men. I don't need to be in a relationship. I don't even have to know his real name. Hell, most times, he doesn't know mine! I am out for one thing and I am quite good at getting it. This has made me rather popular over the years—with men; women, not so much.

It is amazing how easy it is to spot a slut. Even though we don't go around sporting a bright scarlet letter like in the 'olden' days, we do wear it on our sleeve. More accurately, our clothes (or lack of) gives us away every time: the more than ample cleavage; the too-short skirt; the too-tight blouse that shows just a hint of the shocking pink lace bra; the glimpse of a thong as we bend over, teetering on stilettos, showing the top of our stockings... as if we had to do any of that to get our prize.

The makeup provides another layer of masking: carefully applied lipstick with just a hint of gloss; false eyelashes and smouldering shadow; a hint of glitter on the décolletage; sprayed and teased hair; and red nailpolish. What a package! And then there's the scent. As if our pheromones aren't enough to knock over any unassuming man, we load up on a killer fragrance that completely intoxicates those nearby, mesmerizing and luring them into our control for the rest of the night.

You see, when we are on the prowl, we are not looking for Mr. Right. We are looking for Mr. Right Now. That's it. Our ensemble, from head to toe, beckons them near and they are putty in our hands. We can get free drinks, an invitation for fine dining, and then some hot, smokin', no-strings-attached sex. And that is just what we want. A little bit of fun. We're not hurting anyone.

I will admit that every now and then I get a little twinge of guilt, especially when I find out (because I invariably do) that Mr. Right Now actually left my side and went back home to his girlfriend or wife. This is the evidence of the power I have over men when I get my slut on. Have I ever been hurt? No, luckily, but this is all part of the charade that comes with the clothes, the makeup and the perfume. The final layer, you see, is the hardened heart that does not allow Mr. Right to show up and treat me like a Princess. I'm not ready for that yet. I'm just getting what I want and therefore, my heart stays intact. I don't have to worry about letting them know the real me: the Impressive Woman.

I keep my promiscuity as discrete as possible, choosing to frequent bars where travellers land for business trips and visiting bands may be looking to round up a little more mature private audience after the show as opposed to the standard 20-year-old groupie. Ultimately, that's what I feel I am: a man groupie. I love them. I love how they make me feel. And I love what I do to them. But no one needs to know. I don't look or act like this during the weekdays when I'm doing my Impressive-Woman-Thing at work. Most of my friends don't even know this side of me. Keeping this secret is almost as exciting as the charade itself.

What if they knew I am a slut?

I am a Slob

SARA, 31

I joined a group of new mothers when I was on my second maternity leave and it was like a gift from Heaven. Our weekly gatherings were a way for me to stay in touch without the social network that work had provided for so long. I had wondered to myself how I would manage to be at home with two small children without adult conversation for an entire year. Yes, I had my husband to chat with in the evenings when he came home from work, but the quality of that conversation had devolved to pleasantries about how his day was and how many times I change diapers. Really, I couldn't stand to hear him talk about work while my brain was slowly turning to mush. I resented his presence most of the time, especially when he expected me to be Miss Holly Homemaker while he was bringing home the bacon.

Therefore, when the opportunity came to connect with other Impressive Women who just happened to have babies the same age as mine, I jumped at it. Every Monday afternoon, we would compare parenting notes about breastfeeding, introducing baby food, and the newest educational toys for our growing clan. We also dished about our husbands and the lack of intellectual stimulation we were collectively experiencing while away from the workforce. It was like a support group. We always felt better after getting together.

One of the things that particularly inspired me at each meeting was how well-kept all of my new friends' homes were. You see, we alternated homes each week and, because I didn't know any of these ladies prior to being part of the group, I had no idea whether their homes were always so impressive; I just believed it to be so. This is when I came to the stark realization that my new life as the parent of two small children had turned me into a hopeless slob! My greatest anxiety during my second maternity leave had nothing to do with raising children but, more challenging, maintaining some semblance of order in my home when I was in it all the time!

I realized that being home and puttering—seemingly without purpose—chasing around a toddler and various playmates and changing diapers eight times a day, left little time and energy for regular household maintenance. While my husband couldn't figure out what I was doing all day (and, quite frankly, neither could I since my Franklin Covey planner was empty!), I just couldn't keep on top of the laundry, dishes, toys, and books. I was suffering from overwhelm and feared that someone would find out that I wasn't the embodiment of Martha Stewart that I had aspired to be when I had this entire year off to devote to my home. The sad truth was that my house was in disarray most of the time; the dishes only got washed when there were none left for the dinner table; and my son's last pair of underwear in the drawer was the indicator that it was time to do laundry.

The gripping reality was that I had to "get it together" and reclaim my Impressive Woman status by transforming my home into a masterpiece. In order to facilitate this process, I'd make a long list of things to do and organize my day down to the minute. I would cordon off a piece of the house for the children to destroy as I worked myself into a frenzy cleaning carpets, bathrooms, and kitchen while baking muffins and making smoothies for my nine mommy friends. I would have to set timers all over the house to remind myself to feed the children and take a shower before the guests arrived.

Thankfully I only had to do this once every 10-week cycle because I don't know that my sanity would have survived. I'd manage to keep it all together for the three-hour visit and then

I'd collapse from exhaustion and call my husband to get take-out for supper, as I obsessed over what the other mothers must be thinking.

What if they knew I am a slob?

I am an Addict

I don't mean that I'm a crack head. I think it would be pretty hard to pull off the Impressive Woman facade with that issue. What I mean is that I have an addictive personality. Anyone else out there like that? You may call it super-focused, dedicated, and goal-oriented when you are trying to explain your behaviour, like when you are in a job interview and you are asked to list your weaknesses. In the spirit of this confession, I think it is most accurate to describe my addictions as manifestations of *seasonal obsessive compulsive disorder*. Let me explain.

A few months ago, I decided to kick carbs to the curb. That was it. I had had it with the heaviness and the fatigue that seemed to stem from the carbohydrate-heavy diet that was not only packing on pounds around my middle but, I believed, because the media says so, that carbs were the enemy. So off I went to empty my cupboards to the bare bones and consume lean meats, veggies, and well... that's about it. I was an Impressive Woman on a mission. For two weeks. I turned down movie dates because of the temptation of popcorn. I didn't go out with the staff for lunch on Fridays because of the risk of indulging in 'just a few' French fries. I fought hunger pangs and the shakes when I passed the Pizza Hut on the way home each day. I suffered withdrawal every morning when I when to the cereal cupboard out of habit. It didn't take me very long to realize, that my new regimen was not bringing me happiness. Life really is just not as enjoyable without peanut butter bread so...

I switched my obsession to the gym. Since I'm now eating carbs, I have the energy to exercise but I also have the incentive to burn those calories. I'm going to the gym like a maniac. Every spare bit of time, I'm doing leg lifts and sit-ups. I'm taking aerobics classes and walking up the stairs instead of taking the elevator. I'm turning down visits with friends and outings with the kids because I'd rather work up a sweat with a bunch of strangers in a sterile environment full of machines and groovy music. I've started to notice a difference in how my clothes fit but now I'm wondering how I am going to afford a new wardrobe when my waist and butt start getting smaller. Hmmm... perhaps this wasn't such a great idea. I lasted one month.

I'm now getting exercise by redecorating. I usually go on a binge once a year. I purchase new pillows and candles, towels for the bathroom and flowers for the kitchen table. And, just for good measure, I move around all the furniture in each room of my home much to the chagrin of the family who likes everything the way it is, and my friends who have to help out. I draw out new plans, measure it all, and usually decide that I just *have* to have a new table, chair, or ottoman to finish the look. Even though my house isn't getting bigger, I can justify the additional pieces because of how they make me feel. It also satisfies my overwhelming desire to spend money. But that's a bigger story in itself.

Whenever I take on one of these self-improvement projects, everything else suffers. I forget the day-to-day necessities like laundry, meals, and paying bills. I forget to return phone calls and I may be absent from facebook for days. At the outset, I see these choices as beneficial to my overall well-being; as they become my obsession, I realize that my behaviour isn't that healthy after all. I just can't seem to take on something and do it half-way; I commit to the point of self-destruction.

What if they knew I am an addict?

I am Abused

The first time he hit me was when I had come home an hour late after an evening hen party at one of my girlfriend's houses. We were all having such a great time, laughing, drinking wine, and playing Pictionary that I completely lost track of time. I tiptoed into the house, not wanting to disturb my husband who may be asleep since it was now 1:00AM on a Friday. But he wasn't asleep. And, he was already disturbed.

I guess when I look back on it, I shouldn't be that surprised that his violent outbursts became routine after that episode. Now, I don't mean that they happened every other day—it's not like I am a battered wife or anything. I did become aware of patterns of behaviour, however, and I could usually predict when his bad mood was about to teeter over the edge and the abuser would show its ugly face.

My husband had grown up in a verbally abusive household. There wasn't much affection ever shown to him as a child. Knowing this, I was very surprised at how wonderfully attentive he could be, especially when we first started dating in our late teens. He was so in to me. He always complimented me and told me that I was the only girl for him. In hindsight, I recognize the web that he was weaving when he also dropped statements like, "If any guy here looks at you, I'll take him out." When I would try to diffuse the hostility with humour and say, "Sure, you know there's a line up of guys waiting to date me because I am so beautiful," he would look at me with disgust and contempt. In later years, an off-hand comment like that would result in scathing insults about how ugly I was and how no man in his right mind would ever want me. Clearly, there was truth to the latter. *He* wasn't in his right mind.

Sadly, I started to notice a change in my other relationships. Perhaps it was due to the fact that I spent less and less time with my girlfriends. My husband repeatedly referred to them as "man-hating bitches" and, figured that, by association, I would turn into one. I avoided talking about my marriage with anyone and swept under the rug any suggestion that my husband was being controlling. "He just wants the best for me. It makes sense to stay in and save my money for that vacation we are planning," I would sheepishly reply.

That vacation? Yeah, that never happened. The thought of another man looking at my bikini-clad body was enough for him to cancel our trip to Hawaii that we had been planning since we had gotten married six years before. For me, that was the straw that broke the camel's back. When I made up my mind to leave him once and for all, I finally lost control of my emotions. All the repressed rage that I had been feeling for years came out. I think I was near hysteria when I told him I didn't want to go on the trip anyway because my biceps had the marks of his five fingertips emblazoned right there for all the world to see. The anger overshadowed the guilt, embarrassment and shame that I had been carrying around for the duration of our relationship. I knew that I had finally come to the point of no return.

I escaped one night when he was sleeping and, with the help of friends, I've been able to get my life in order. Still, they don't know my secret. They just think, like so many other couples who get together when they are young, that we drifted apart. They didn't know that I worked hard every day to arrange my clothes so no one would ever know how this Impressive Woman had gotten trapped in a marriage with an abusive husband.

What if they knew I am abused?

I am Broke

When I was young, I always had money. I was that kid who always had enough allowance left over at the end of the week to treat my not-so-wealthy friends to an ice cream at Dairy Queen. My family wasn't wealthy, by any means, but they instilled in me a significant respect for money and its power to give you the life that you desire. My parents, in fact, were quite frugal. They believed in saving for short- and long-term goals and never relying on debt for purchases smaller than a vehicle. This relationship with money shaped my own perceptions and buying decisions for a very long time.

Through my university years, I always came home with enough spending money to get me through the summer. I was not a big spender but never had to turn down the opportunity to go to a concert or weekend away because I was short of change. Getting married didn't change this either because I selected a partner who was even more frugal. For years, I never knew when payday was. I rarely checked the balance in my bank account because there was always enough money to cover my expenses, including the recommended portion that was being redirected to retirement savings accounts.

All that has changed. A number of life events–including a divorce, new home, and change in employment status–has found me relying heavily on debt and with a constant angst when faced with invitations to travel, eat out, and entertain because I just don't know how I am going to pay for it all. I used to think that my financial security was one of my most attractive qualities. Now I go through pains to avoid talking about money and try to live in such a way that no one would ever suspect that I don't know where the next mortgage payment will surface. I am ashamed and I am embarrassed.

I do what I can to minimize my spending on entertainment; I've cut back on movies, restaurants, and concerts. I am more careful about my driving; the price of gas is astronomical these days. I ration food like I'm preparing for an ice storm. See, these are all tactics I can take to stretch my dollars *without anyone having to know*. I am proud of the choices that I have made in these times of scarcity. I do hope my fortune turns around soon. I worry about the short-term as much as I used to worry about saving for the children's education.

I think my parents are worried about me, too. You'd be worried about your child, wouldn't you? Gee, thanks! Let's add some guilt to how I am feeling, too! As a grown woman, I don't want anyone to worry about me. As an Impressive Woman, I certainly don't want anyone to pity me or view me as a charity case. Above all, I don't want my children to know that I am suffering financially. The guilt I feel will not be passed on to my children, even if it means that I have to "rob Peter to pay Paul" for a while longer. I will take them on vacations and buy presents for them because that's what they have come to expect from their mother, the Impressive Woman. I don't want to let them down. I'm also afraid that the invitations would stop coming and that people would keep their distance because they don't want to make me feel bad.

What if they knew I am broke?

I am Angry

Life is not fair. Bad things happen to good people and, frankly, I've had enough of it. They say that nice guys finish last; well, nice girls don't even get to play half of the time. Is there any wonder this Impressive Woman is angry? I'm done with being nice. I'm angry and I'm going to show it. Well, maybe... I must consider my image, after all.

That's part of what makes me angry. If I blow off steam and someone sees me, I risk having my reputation as an Impressive Woman tarnished beyond repair. Is that fair? Heck, no! If a guy blows his stack at the office, people are likely to brush it off, saying that he's under a lot of pressure or that the boss has been riding him. Listen, I can guarantee you that no man has ever been under as much pressure as an Impressive Woman. They couldn't handle a quarter of what we do. That's why they are in awe of us. That's why they don't know how to communicate with us. They don't get it. They don't get us.

Does that ever make me angry! Why? Because, like it or not, men still have a controlling interest in the way the planet is run. There are a few exceptions but out of all the decision makers that I deal with in my life—personally and professionally—90 percent are men. We, the Impressive Women, must learn to get along and make success happen despite our differences. There we go again... bridging the gap, making concessions, turning a blind eye, and biting our tongues so that egos don't get bruised and business deals happen. We are the creators of peace. It makes me so angry.

I really hate it when hard-working people get overlooked because someone else was just a little shinier; or worse, when the other person was just a little *whinier*. I get so angry when the "squeaky wheel gets the grease". What about everyone else who comes in and does a good day's work without complaining that there isn't enough money in the budget for fancy staplers and graph paper? What about the person who never takes a sick day? What about the person who always stays late to ensure the payroll gets processed? Where are the accolades and promotions for these diligent souls? Oh yeah, they went to the "brown-noser" in accounting that we hired last year out of university. What is the world coming to?

The straw that broke the camel's back last week was when my friend was diagnosed with cancer. She is the sweetest woman you could ever meet. She is loving and caring, smart and bright. She doesn't deserve to be subjected to the tests and treatment that she will undergo in the next few months. It makes me so angry! I hate to see her in pain and I definitely don't want to add to her suffering or stress.

So, for the sake of my friend, I will keep my anger to myself. Perhaps I'll journal about it so that it doesn't get trapped inside me and make me a walking time bomb. I will put on the face of the Impressive Woman and be there for her. Bad things happen to good people. It makes us angry. That's ok. We still have to deal.

What if they knew I am angry?

I am a Procrastinator

You've heard it before. Perhaps you have even said it: There are not enough hours in the day! For a master procrastinator like me, there is great comfort in this popular excuse. It gives me all the leverage I need to delay, delay, delay. Like every Impressive Woman, I have a massive to-do list every day. The many hats that I wear leave little breathing room in my busy life. There is always more to do. That is why I can always find a *legitimate* reason to not do those things which I like the least.

I make a master to-do list at the beginning of every week. It is quite comprehensive and includes a myriad of reminders centered around family, friends, work, home, health, and fitness. I love making lists: I am a chronic list-maker, in fact. While I love the feeling of checking things off my list, there are certain items—like taxes and household budgets, expense reports and cleaning the refrigerator—that lose their priority against fun like coffee with friends, play-dates with the kids, and date night with my honey. Would I rather spend time doing the former when I have the latter, much more enjoyable, options? Heck, no! I'll just move those nasty items to another day on my calendar and play away.

With this philosophy squarely in the back of my mind, I made a startling and humbling discovery one day: I had moved one item to the start of every week's to-do list for three months in a row!! There should be some kind of medal for that, don't you think? It's quite impressive! See, *just like that* I can justify my procrastination! It's not like I was deliberately putting it off; I am a busy woman. I am in demand by many people. I have obligations and invitations.

There are work commitments, family responsibilities, and social functions that require my attention.

I have been caught in this trap a few times but I just don't seem to learn my lesson. Once, I got a call from the day care centre because I forgot to update my expired credit card on file; the kids were on the brink of expulsion because of my lack of diligence. That was embarrassing. I have had to quickly rinse out a pair of pantyhose before going to work because I just didn't get around to doing laundry in the past week. Luckily, no third party had to know about that! I have received repeated reminders from the taxation office that I will continue to accumulate interest if I don't soon pay off my annual bill. That one really hurts. "Yes, officer," I feel like saying, "I will be right down." But then, something more interesting flies across my desk and I'm distracted (and accruing interest) once again.

All nighters, I have pulled them—at work, at school, and even when company is coming. There's nothing like a rigid deadline and the expectations of others to kick this procrastinator's butt into action. Truly, I don't want anyone else to be seriously affected by my destructive behaviour. I really don't want anyone to blame me for projects being late or over budget. I don't want anyone pointing their fingers at me in judgment. I want everyone to go along thinking that I am an Impressive Woman: I am the woman they can depend on to "take care of business"; I am the woman who has got all her ducks in a row; I am the woman who can handle anything thrown at her because she is so organized.

What if they knew I am a procrastinator?

I am Jealous

I genuinely want the people in my life to be happy but sometimes, I find myself being completely jealous. When my friend fell in love, I smiled and hugged her. She had been waiting so long for that 'someone special' to sweep her off her feet and treat her like an Impressive Woman. But when I got home, I sat quietly and cried. I was so jealous! I mean, I've been waiting A LOT longer than her for Prince Charming to arrive. Why should she have all the happiness???

Then there is my friend with the beautifully appointed home. I wish I had the time and the money to be able to buy a home like that, and then decorate it so it looks like it came straight out of the pages of *Better Homes and Gardens*. I would have a great big deck on the back of the house with wrought-iron tables overflowing with flowering plants. I'd have a covered gazebo with a hot tub that I'd use every night. I'd have a big umbrella perched on top of a flowery lounger where I could read in the shade. *Just like my friend's*. Yes, it's what I've always wanted. I am happy for her success but *man*, am I ever jealous!

I have a co-worker who just got a promotion. Truthfully, she really deserved it. She works hard and is always ready to go "above and beyond" to solve a customer problem. Due to her efforts, she'll be enjoying a raise, a new corner office, and an assistant. These are the things of which I have dreamed since joining the company. I follow her example as best I can but there never seems to be an opportunity for me to advance and I struggle to balance my feelings of happiness for her with my thoughts that, *if something were to 'happen' to her*, perhaps… just maybe, I'd get that corner office.

It's shameful to admit that my jealousy can turn dark. My imagination conjures accidents that will befall these lucky people. It's shocking but it's true. If I can think awful things about my friends, imagine what dangers lurk in my mind when I'm in a jealous rage because of someone I don't like!

This happened once (yes, only once) when a guy I was dating was getting unsolicited attention from another woman, and was *enjoying it way too much*. When I tried to bring it up politely, he just shrugged it off, not really acknowledging my feelings. Unfortunately, the attention from this woman became much more overt, demonstrating her brazenness, and I confronted him again. Can you believe that he actually got mad at *me* for making a big deal about it? I told him that she was deliberately trying to break us up and unless he dealt with it, I would be making my displeasure known in a way she wouldn't soon forget. The look in my eyes told him I meant business so he did contact her and the relationship ended. Theirs, and ours shortly after.

I found myself so consumed with jealousy in that relationship that I realized there had to be a reason. My insecurity was bad enough but his flirtatious ways were really quite disrespectful to me. Once I wised up and saw him for who he really was, I decided that my jealous tendencies could be better spent on someone who would treat me like the Impressive Woman that I am.

What have I learned as I have come to terms with my jealousy? Well, I know what I want, and that's a good thing! The "green monster" is not a pleasant aspect of my personality so I'm going to do my best to use it as a barometer to identify what I really want in life. Then I'll go after it as any Impressive Woman would and then, maybe, people will be jealous of me!

What if they knew I am jealous?

I am Disappointed

The only way to avoid disappointment is to not set expectations. This is very hard when you are accustomed to working hard to get what you want and giving more than 100% in everything you do, as an Impressive Woman. But I try. I try because I have learned that not everyone has the same motivation, the same values or the same core beliefs. Still, when you work with someone toward the same goals, it is disappointing when they don't deliver as you would like.

I have tried to be crystal clear about my intentions from the outset and the various roles and responsibilities of each member of the team. There is always room for misinterpretation, however, because everyone's perspective is different. Where there is room for speculation, you can be sure it will happen that you're not on the same page and you don't see eye to eye about how things should happen, in what timeframe, and you will differ in your opinion of the best approach to solve problems. Oftentimes, the outcome is not going to be in your favour. Or, so I've experienced.

I am routinely disappointed. While, intellectually, I understand that my priorities are not the same as those around me, I struggle to understand why all people don't go to work with the desire to give 100% (at least). Why don't we all just try our best? Why are some people okay with mediocrity? I don't get it and because of that–because of my lack of understanding–I am continually disappointed in the performance of others.

This doesn't just apply to work. It also applies to relationships. I've been in so many where I am left feeling that I was always the one giving more. I am the one who cooperates, compromises, and concedes. I am the one who considers the feelings of others and accommodates their schedules, stressors and needs. When is it going to be my time? When will I feel that those same considerations are made for me? When will I feel like the playing field is finally level? It feels like an uphill climb... and it is tiring.

I suppose that I could alienate myself completely. I could take a job where I was completely independent. Is there such a thing? Well, perhaps I could investigate and find one that has the *minimal* dependence on other people to make it succeed. I know that if I have as much control as possible, my probability of success is quite high. It is only when my flow is interrupted by other people–managers, coworkers, clients, family, friends, traffic cops–that my life spirals downward and my disappointment goes up.

Do you know who feels the brunt of my disappointment? Me. It doesn't make sense when you think about it. If I'm the only one I can count on, then why would I ever be disappointed in myself? Shouldn't I be my biggest supporter? The truth is that I'm not perfect and, for that reason, I am disappointed in myself. There are always ways that I can improve. I don't always have the right answer and many times I make mistakes. As an Impressive Woman, I have high expectations of myself and I let myself down over and over again.

What if they knew I am disappointed?

I am a Bully

BILLIE JEAN, 21

When I know I am right, I want everyone to follow me. I am a dominant personality and my assertiveness sometimes turns into full-fledged aggression. That's when I become a bully. Put someone in front of me who doesn't have a spine and who has the slightest potential for standing in the way of me getting what I want, and I will make it known that I am the one who will win. I will fight for what I believe is right. I will crush those that threaten me into submission and I will reign supreme!

I don't behave like this all the time. I am the Impressive Young Woman on campus. In the dorm, I am very popular and my door is always open for a chat and a few laughs. Come into my room and you are welcome, if you want to watch the show I am watching or dance along to the music. Just don't ask me to change the channel or, for Heaven's sake, don't do it without asking me. Normally, this unwritten rule is respected and I don't have to get pushy to get what I want. I tend to like the stuff that is popular so that helps. I do think that some of the quieter girls on my floor are intimidated by me. They don't usually say too much. It's probably because we don't have anything in common. We don't dress the same; we don't read the same books; we don't do the same things on the weekends. They don't usually knock on my door.

In class, people admire me because I generally get the most attention from my professors. I am not afraid to speak up in class and will debate anyone on a subject that is important to me. I don't like to lose, however, and while that makes me work hard to know my stuff before entering an argument, it also fuels my aggression and sometimes the results aren't pretty.

31

I have been known to make things personal when I fear I will lose a debate. When it looks as though my opponent is winning over the majority of the audience, I will make comments that question the other person's credibility. It is always my intention to be somewhat covert in my attempts at distraction. After all, I am considered the Impressive Young Woman and would not want anyone to judge me in a tainted light. I feel like I am serving a higher good when I dominate because of my superior knowledge and skills. So, I will suggest that he or she doesn't have all their facts straight and undermine their expertise. I will even change the subject when I feel desperate, and ask personal questions, especially if I know them well enough to say something really embarrassing. This deflects attention from the debate and makes me look like the more powerful speaker. Am I proud of this behaviour? No. But I would rather be the one giving out the punishment than receiving. And I will not lose if I can help it.

What if they knew I am a bully?

I am Frustrated

FRAN, 56

As I get older, it seems as though my patience is thinning along with my skin and hair. The list of my pet peeves is growing and I have to constantly be on my toes, watching what I say and do so that people don't realize that this Impressive Woman could snap at any moment... especially if I am in the presence of someone who is stupid. I hate stupid people!! I detest being subjected to their screws ups. They frustrate me to no end.

In order to get this out of my system, I have compiled a list of some of the things that frustrate me the most:

- Stupid people (already covered)
- Inefficiency
- Lack of planning
- Indecision
- Files that are not kept current
- Technology that is outdated when you buy it
- Restaurant servers who don't replenish my empty water glass
- Empty toilet paper rolls
- Less than a glass of milk left in the container
- Cosmetic companies who discontinue my favourite product
- People who stand in long lines for tickets and don't know what they want when they get to the front
- Cheque cashing at the grocery store
- Drivers who got their licenses from a Cracker Jack Box

- Dirty dishes in the office sink
- Slipping bra straps
- Inaccurate weather forecasts
- Pushovers
- Whiners and complainers who do nothing to change their situations
- Price checks at the register
- Insurance companies who disallow your claim for a pre-existing condition
- White socks and black shoes
- Pantyhose that run
- Snow plows that come just when you have finished shovelling the driveway
- Apples that are bruised by the time you get home from the grocery store
- Pillar candles that warp into nasty shapes as they burn
- Having to buy 40 tampons when all you need is one
- Cat hair—*on everything*
- One bathroom in a home with a teenage girl
- Passport photos—you're not allowed to smile anymore, don't you know
- And, of course... When the toilet seat is left UP!

Thanks for letting me vent. I feel so much better. In fact, I feel like a normal, Impressive Woman.

What if they knew I am frustrated?

I am Fat

Sure, I may look good to you but for many, many years I have hated practically every part of my body. From my feet to my hair, I have had serious bouts of self-loathing as it relates to my looks. I have covered up my flaws with clothes and make-up in order to look like an Impressive Woman and walk confidently out the door, but some days, that isn't so easy. There are days, upon peering into the mirror, the negative talk can be so loud, it makes me want to go back to bed and put a pillow over my head to drown it out. Imagine!

The biggest issue I have been dealing with since I was a little girl is that I am fat. Fat is not a word I would normally use, but in the spirit of this confession, I must face facts. I am not just big-boned, like my grandmother would say afflicts all the women in our family, but I am fat. I have always carried excess weight around my thighs and my middle. All attempts to get rid of this fat have left me with a sinking feeling that it is simply *who I am meant to be in the world* because it will never go away.

I go to the gym, albeit sporadically. What do you expect? What kind of confidence level does a person have to have to exercise in front of full length mirrors? Add to that an audience of people that are, of course, more fit than you are, and you have a major anxiety-inducing situation. So, I only go to the gym on days when I am feeling skinnier than usual, I look really great, and I have energy. These days don't come along that often, but when they do, I try to get the most out of them.

The day after I go to the gym is not usually one of those days. I ache. I feel exhausted. I feel fatter. I am reminded, at

35

the gym, how out-of-shape I have become. And I really don't need the reminding. I get winded walking up the stairs in my house, shovelling the front steps, and bring groceries into the kitchen. Luckily, I live alone so no one has to witness this. I am embarrassed for myself. When I am asked to partake in any kind of activity that involves physical exertion—like skiing, hiking, kayaking—I always have an excuse. People buy it because I'm an Impressive Woman, with a lot of my plate. What if they knew that the reason I wasn't going—as much as I'd love to—is because I am too fat?

When I look at pictures from my past, all I see are the rolls around my middle and my double chin. I have tried every different kind of diet and exercise plan and, sure, I have lost weight, but what I find amazing is that when I was at my smallest, I remember that I still felt fat every single day. It makes me want to cry. Oh, how I long to see my collarbone and my hipbones, to have seamless curves under a tight dress or sweater instead of bumps and jiggly bits. So, I do my best and people say, "You look great." Yeah, right. I'm not convinced.

I long to have the confidence in my body that I possess in the workplace or at home, raising my children, but the moment I have to undress in front of anyone or observe my body in the mirror, I get tense and feel completely inadequate. I have been in relationships with men and have insisted on having the lights turned out during lovemaking for fear of turning him off. It has even prevented me from being on top!!

What if they knew I am fat?

I am Needy

Right now, I feel like I am being shut out of my boyfriend's life. It is true that he has a lot on his mind. There are significant pressures at work, his divorce is not yet finalized, and his health hasn't been the greatest. I want to help but he just shuts me out. I want to put my arms around him and tell him it will all be okay.

But that's what I want, too. I want a hug. I feel neglected. I feel helpless.

When we are together, we avoid any serious conversation. We don't talk about his work; we certainly don't talk about his divorce; and his health is completely off-limits. You would think that we'd talk about me, then, right? Wrong. Since we aren't allowed to talk about his issues, we aren't allowed to talk about mine either. I need a shoulder right now. My boss is pushing me so hard, my coworkers are not pulling their weight, and I think I deserve a raise. I want to talk to my boyfriend about these things; I want his opinion—I value his insight.

Nonetheless, when he has his own stuff to deal with, I don't want to burden him with my problems. One time, I got angry when he didn't sympathize with my situation, and asked him, "Why don't you understand?" Then, I realized that I hadn't shared anything with him. I was fighting a losing battle.

What I really wanted to say was, "I need validation. I need attention. I need affection. I need a shoulder and a pair of ears." Of course, on the day that I finally stepped up and told him what I wanted from him, my boyfriend of one-year replied, "You are too needy."

The truth hurts, I guess. It cuts like a knife. I didn't feel much like an Impressive Woman when he said that. Come to think of it, I didn't ever feel like an Impressive Woman when I was in his company. I have felt alone in this relationship and, until he gives me what I need, I will replay every word of our last conversation in my mind, convincing myself that I have done something to warrant his negligence. That makes me even needier—for his assurance.

Maybe needy people are created because they are not getting what they need from the people around them. Maybe needy people are not demanding at all; they just aren't successful at communicating. Maybe needy people give too much and ask for too little in return. Maybe needy people just *need* a little bit more than they are getting.

This stigma of being a needy woman is a hard one to shake. Try listing *that* as one of your qualities on your Plenty-of-Fish dating profile. A needy girlfriend is that last thing that guys want. Can you blame them? Would I want to hang out with me if I was constantly whining about not getting enough attention? Would I want to have someone clinging on to me when we walk downtown? Would I want someone else's life to revolve around mine because they don't have a sense of who they are without me?

With those facts in mind, I venture out on the single scene again. (You didn't think I was going to stick around with Mr. Brick Wall, did you?) I will keep my needy self on lock-down. I will do my best to attract a man who is worthy of this Impressive Woman, and use my Needy Natalie alter-ego as a guidepost to let me know when I've gone astray.

What if they knew I am needy?

I am Vain

Why is it that when I go to home decor stores, I instinctively go to the bathroom section? Because that's where the most mirrors per square foot of floor space are located! I size myself up and down in every washroom, as I pretend to admire the finish on vanities and faucets. Pretty crazy, but it is true. I love mirrors because I love to look at myself. I especially love those that are in surprising, yet convenient places.

Here are my top five:

- **Coming off the plane at the airport.** Long windowed corridors are like mirrors so they get my vote, too. They provide a warning that *I must first go to the washroom* to fix my wrinkled clothes and puffy hair before descending to the baggage carrousel where my honey awaits.
- **Fancy restaurant washroom.** Full length mirrors allow me to check for spaghetti stains on my clothes after I finish brushing and flossing and using the cotton facecloths provided. In addition to reapplying my lip gloss, I can also see if my belt really needs adjusting because it sure feels like it does!
- **Upscale retail dressing rooms.** Tri-fold mirrors are awesome because I can *really* see what's going on with my butt. (It is my favourite feature yet, the one I see least often because I don't have one of these mirrors in my own home.)

- **The gym locker.** Smiling at my freshly showered self, I congratulate myself on yet another perfect workout as I stay on target for my fitness goals this year.
- **The mirror on my desk by my phone.** I use it to ramp up my friendliness on customer calls. (They can tell when you're not smiling, you know.) Gosh, I have a great smile!

Looking this good doesn't come by accident. Although I am blessed with a genetically good butt and perky boobs, gravity seems to be attacking me as I get older and I have to spend just a little longer taking care of my face, hair and body to maintain my youthful appearance. How much time do I spend each day? That's a secret I will never reveal!

I do recommend to other Impressive Women to take pride in their appearance. You never get a second chance to make a first impression so I believe it requires a necessary investment of time, energy and money. Get a gym membership. Maintain those locks and nails. Whiten those teeth. Slap on the sunscreen like it's going out of style. Protect your eyes. Wear classic clothes that fit well, accentuate your assets and camouflage your jiggly bits.

It's not easy being this gorgeous, but it has its benefits and I intend to keep raking them in!

What if they knew I am vain?

I am Scatter-Brained

Juggling is a feat I have never quite managed. Juggling, that is, as we know it from the circus. When it comes to wearing many hats, balancing the needs of others, and keeping multiple projects going simultaneously, I am a pro. As an Impressive Woman, multi-tasking is part of the shtick. Usually, you get better at it with practice. You know that if you want something done you ask a busy person (aka an Impressive Woman) because that's how we roll. I can tack on another couple of items to the daily to-do list without batting an eye. But don't ask me "on the fly" when I don't have pen and paper (or mobile phone) in hand because, my big secret is that I am completely and utterly scatter-brained. My brain has slowly turned to mush over the years and if it's not written down, it ain't getting done!

Luckily, I am a chronic list-maker. I have been since about the age of 10. To me, there is nothing more exhilarating than taking a crisp, clean piece of paper (white or otherwise—I'm not particular on that matter) and recording an awesome to-do list. Actually, there is... and that is *checking off* the items on the list!

While I have always been a list-maker, I have not always needed to rely on it so heavily. Since having children, my plate has gotten incredibly full and I just don't trust that my memory will keep me going from 6:00AM to midnight without overlooking something major. Paper or electronic, the list is my saving grace. It keeps me focused. It keeps me on task and on time. I am incredibly productive when I have my list in hand. And, as I said before, I can add to it throughout the day, and I will still get it all done.

My list makes me invincible! It makes me feel like an Impressive Woman.

I also love calendars. I feel so empowered when I look at a fresh month with all its clean blocks just waiting for me to record the many obligations that I manage. I love calendars so much that I have one in every room of my house. I don't record stuff on all of them, but I secretly want to mark them all up because of the validation it provides: I am an Impressive Woman. All you have to do is look at my calendar for the proof!

My 13-year-old son doesn't think any of this makes sense. In fact, he doesn't believe in writing anything down nor does he read calendars. He knows what day it is and what day it will be tomorrow, he tells me with confidence. He knows what needs to be done and he gets it done. He doesn't need to check anything off. Who is this child? Did he really come from me?

It is my son who reminds me, incessantly, of my failing memory. He'll recount stories of years past when so-and-so did this-and-that and will end with the knowing, "Remember, Mom?" I think he does this deliberately to embarrass me and highlight my flaws; either that, or he is touting his superior mental capacity. One of these days, I may surprise him and say, "Well, yes, I do. I remember it well." And hopefully, he won't realize that I'm lying!

What if they knew I am scatter-brained?

I am Insecure

Do you remember what it was like to walk into school on the first day of junior high in September sporting your new clothes and backpack? I do. The anticipation nearly killed me. I definitely didn't sleep well the night before. I could barely eat breakfast that morning. As I'd walk the 15 minutes to school, my stomach would do flip-flops. When I entered the building, my face would flush and I'd brace myself for the news I had been thinking about for weeks.

Was I concerned about what class schedule I would have? Did I care who my homeroom teacher would be? Was I anxious about what boy would have the locker next to mine? No, no, no. The anxiety was all about what I was wearing. I needed desperately to hear what the other girls in my class thought about my new outfit. I was always meticulously dressed, and in the latest fashions, but my sense of self was completely dependent on the validation of a few people, in the bathroom, on the first day of school.

The pressure was incredible. Luckily, I passed with flying colors. They liked how I dressed and styled my hair. I walked a little taller out of that bathroom and sailed through the day an Impressive Young Woman. My confidence was an 11 out of 10 and it showed in how I carried myself and communicated... until the next big test: Friday night's dance. *What will I wear?*

Did that bring back memories for you? The odd thing is that, with very few modifications, I could have been telling that story about last weekend, when I went to a networking function. I took significant pains to dress in the latest style to convey to every person I met that I am an Impressive Woman. I had the same problems sleeping and eating, and could even feel the flushed cheeks accompanying me into the event. I didn't relax until the hostess remarked how terrific I looked and asked where I bought my new boots.

Why is it that I have been dependent on the words of others before forming my own opinion of myself? When I look in the mirror, I cannot make a distinction whether I look good or not. My life is in limbo until someone gives the nod of approval. I have been lucky, I'll admit. I have usually gotten "the nod". Because of that, I have felt good about myself for the most part. But there have been times when it was not the case and my biggest fear is that my daughter will develop these same insecurities and NOT get the nod like I did.

I think I was her age when my insecurity began. I was about 10 years old when I started to take an interest in how I was dressing and styling my hair. I started liking boys and had a number of girlfriends with whom I spent time outside of school. We always talked about fashion and cosmetics. I became so entrenched in the group that I couldn't imagine what life would be like if they didn't approve of me.

One day, sadly, I got a taste of it. It wasn't the first day of school, but another significant day in the school calendar—picture day. I arrived, proudly wearing a new dress and braids. When I went to the bathroom to check my hair before lining up for the photographer, I noticed that one of my braids had come undone. I had no choice but to unravel them and wear my hair down, in great big waves. I still thought it looked nice, but my girlfriends didn't and they laughed so much that *everyone* noticed. My feelings were hurt but I wouldn't let them see. I joked about it along with them and promised I'd get a retake of my photos next month.

I did get my picture redone but secretly kept the original proofs. The proofs remind me of the day I gave my power away. I wish I could get it back. Perhaps I'll tell this story to my daughter.

What if they knew I am insecure?

I am Submissive

You wouldn't think that an Impressive Woman like me would ever be meek and mild. You'd never think that I would cower in fear. You'd never think that I, who had always been so independent-minded and keen on advancing my own agenda would be stopped short by someone I hardly knew. You wouldn't believe it, but it is true. Sadly, I have been in situations before that have rendered me quite submissive. There is no better way to describe my behaviour.

"Yes Sir." I'd cringe and nearly throw up every time I was conscious enough to realize what I was saying. The place where I held my first management position exposed me to this side of me. I was 24 years old and had never, ever been submissive before. In fact, as an Impressive Woman, I had been known to walk right on over people who displayed such behaviour. I found it offensive that people could be so insecure and docile. I had no problem speaking up at any point in time to whatever audience I had, and clearly express my opinions without fear of retribution. But all that changed one day when I was introduced to my new Regional Manager.

This man was like a god to me. He had the title I wanted and the swagger. And, he knew he was hot stuff. Unfortunately, he used his position power for evil instead of good and I soon came to loathe him and the way he managed our team. Specifically, he was condescending and patronizing. He made a point to ridicule the smallest infractions in front of the entire team and admonish you like you were a 5-year-old who had stolen a playmate's toy. It was insulting and degrading. I saw that he was like this with

45

everyone. Thank goodness he didn't visit our office very often. I felt dirty after his visits; I felt embarrassed for losing myself in his arrogance. I thought, *"What has become of me?"* Why wasn't I stepping up to protect myself and the other members of my team? I had lost all gumption in the face of this man.

I was a spineless, gutless, sissy. I was so embarrassed. After several months, I could no longer tolerate his influence and, after an incident that left me questioning my future in the industry, I decided to move on.

I left that job primarily because I was ashamed of the person I had become working for this man. I left without another job to go to. Yes, it was *that* bad. Within a few months, after reading countless self-help books and taking a *Dale Carnegie* course, I slowly regained my sense of self. Life resumed as I had originally planned. I got a better job and swiftly moved up another corporate ladder. The world was humming along quite well for this Impressive Woman until one day...

I was sitting in an airport, on my way home from a business trip, when out of the corner of my eye, I spotted him. Yes, that former Regional Manager of mine was 20 meters away. Seeing his face transported me back three years in time and effectively turned me into a puddle of mush. I closed my laptop and hurried off to the ladies' room where I lost myself in gigantic sobs. What power had I given over to this man that he could rattle me years later? Thank goodness I was travelling alone... and we were not on the same flight! It took several days to get over the incident. What am I talking about? I'm still not over it!

What if they knew I am submissive?

I am in Pain

No, really. I have been managing chronic pain for more than three decades now. I really don't know what it's like to be pain-free. Uh... wait a minute, that's not entirely true. I believe I had three days in 2007 and two in 2009. Sorry.

What is it like to wake up in the morning and feel fully rested and ready to jump out of bed and take on the day? I don't know. What I do know is what it's like to wake up happy and feeling wonderful about myself and the possibilities that lie ahead, and to have a body that doesn't respond in kind. Each morning, it takes several minutes before I can even move. And, always, there is pain. I swear sometimes I can actually hear my joints creaking as I move tentatively to the shower. Hot water is my saviour.

If I need to get moving quickly, a shower is a must. If I have the luxury of a few hours before my first outing of the day, I will wait. I will putter around, move ever-so-gingerly and settle into my "special" chair–the one that provides me with exactly the right amount of support in exactly the right spots where I can enjoy my cup of tea and read the newspaper. When it's time to rise, the next challenge is upon me, but I've been able to relax my mind enough that it isn't nearly as difficult as getting out of bed. I hoist myself up, being careful to inhale deeply and exhale fully to minimize the discomfort and distract myself from what I am actually doing: getting out of the chair.

Even though it is ever-present, I don't like to take medication for the pain. For those of you whose bouts of pain come in the form of wine-induced headaches or work-out induced strains, you likely don't understand why I don't just take an aspirin. I, myself, wonder sometimes if I'm just being a martyr. I have tried many, many forms of therapy–physical and otherwise–to alleviate the pain. I have seen doctors, chiropractors, physiotherapists, acupuncturists, naturopaths, nutritionists, energy healers, and psychologists, to name just a few. The results have been negligible, and sometimes, the pain gets worse. Now, don't get me wrong. All of these professionals were wonderful and I believe in their work. But, for me, none of these therapies has relieved me of my pain. That's why I wonder if it isn't time to give in to the pharmaceuticals. How would it change me? What would life be like without the pain?

That leads me to another issue: self-identity. Because I have had the pain so long, it has essentially become part of who I am. If I didn't have pain to limit me, I wouldn't have any excuse for not doing more. I am already doing so much! I don't know if I can handle the expectations that would be placed on me if I was healthy! It is fair to say that I have been using my disability as a crutch. I've had enough time to think about it. Perhaps that's the real reason why the therapies don't work–because I won't allow it! Being healthy would be too much of a departure from life as I know it, that I am actually *afraid to get better*!

Most people, when they meet me, see an Impressive Woman; they don't know that I am in pain. They don't know that the high heels I am wearing are driving stakes of shooting pain up through my legs. They don't know that my hips hurt from standing, my back aches from sitting, and that my head hurts when I lie down (not that I usually do that in front of them.). They don't know that when I put in a full day of work, I need to recover–sometimes for an entire day–depending on how physically demanding my work has been. They don't know that travelling knocks the crap right out of me! Why don't they know? Because it is my weakness and I'm not prepared to let it stop me from being an Impressive Woman. Not in this lifetime.

What if they knew I am in pain?

I am Lost

I'm going around in circles in my mind and have nothing to show for my efforts at the end of the day. I don't have a purpose. I bury myself in reality TV shows because I am not compelled to do anything else with my time. If it weren't for all the obligations that are imposed on me by the roles I play, I probably wouldn't go out the door. And those obligations, I'm afraid to say, I perform with little enthusiasm; my heart is no longer in it.

This all started when I lost my job. I am a career-driven Impressive Woman. At a young age, there was no doubt that I would be climbing a corporate ladder as soon as I was able. I hopped off to university with a full scholarship and graduated at the top of my class. I had multiple job offers to consider upon graduation and chose the one that would give me the greatest opportunity for advancement. By 26, I had really hit my stride.

Everyone in the company knew of my work ethic, unparalleled for such a young person, especially in the company of my Gen-Y cohort. I was the first one to arrive in the morning and the last one to leave. Whenever there was a pressing deadline or a client emergency, I could always be counted on to pull a late night or work on the weekends. I made sure that everyone knew of my commitment to the success of *my* department and *my* company.

Yes, I felt like they were *mine*. I believed that I was such an integral part of the organization that it wouldn't be able to function without me. Certainly I believed that letting me go was next to unthinkable. It really wasn't sane. But, it happened—without warning and without fanfare.

I did receive a compensation package but it wasn't the greatest given that I had little tenure. My stellar performance and many hours of unpaid overtime clearly didn't amount to much once the company was done with me. I started to question my motives, my values, my existence. What was it all for if this was how I would be treated in the end? My life had become meaningless. I had no purpose.

My reason for being had been taken out from under me. There was no regard paid to my well-being from the company for which I had worked so hard. I was actually shocked that they would treat me this way. This was my rude introduction to the corporate world. My idealistic view of the employee-employer relationship had been dramatically altered and I was left alone to wallow.

So here I sit at the ripe old age of 28. It has been two months and I just don't know what to do with myself. I apply for jobs but I'm so jaded that I don't want to commit. Sometimes I blow the interview because I'm afraid that if I like the company too much, I'll get back into the same patterns and get shafted again. I have lost my drive. I have lost my ambition. Really, I have lost my sense of self.

Who would have believed that this would have ever happened to me? I'm quite embarrassed about it all. When my parents call, I tell them I'm fine. When my friends want to go out, I cancel at the last minute. I can't bear to hear their questions or see the sympathy in their eyes. I know I have let them down. If *I* couldn't make a success out of myself, perhaps all hope is lost, just like me.

What if they knew I am lost?

I am Overwhelmed

OLIVE, 45

Yes, I am an Impressive Woman. And before that, I was an Impressive Girl. I have always been one of those people that everyone revered because I looked like I was untouchable. You know what I mean... I was good at most things that I tried and *I tried everything*: music, sports, arts, school, boys. I had many friends and, therefore, many social opportunities. I knew many people and most of them thought that I was the epitome of success. That didn't change as I grew older and took on the roles of university student, career woman, wife, and mother. But as those new hats added up, I didn't let go of much. I continued to volunteer, spend time with friends and family, and push myself to carry it all without breaking a sweat.

Until one day, when I crashed. Actually, it happened a little more regularly than "one day" but when it did, it was usually quite dramatic, and I hid it from the public eye. I mean, *What if they knew that I didn't have it all under control? What would people say if their idea of success was dashed by this so-called Impressive Woman? Would their sense of hope be crushed?* That's a lot of pressure. As if I didn't have enough already!

I feel so overwhelmed with all that there is to do and the pressure to deliver with perfection. I have to have the cleanest house, the best-behaved children, the most fulfilling career, the happiest marriage, the highest yielding stock portfolio... and the list goes on and on. Each day I consult my lengthy to-do list (my saving grace to managing the roles I play) with a quickening heart rate as I race the clock to get it all done before bed. If I don't get through all the items on the list before the day is done, I have a

51

stern talk with myself as I guiltily add them to tomorrow's list. When this happens several days in a row, I can be certain that a crash is heading my way.

I don't know if it's tied to my menstrual cycle or the moon (same thing, really) or what, but I do know that on a regular basis, my capacity to keep all the balls in the air fails miserably and I just want to curl up into a ball and let someone else take over. The problem with that is... *to whom would I delegate all that I do?* Not only would no one else do it like me, or as well as me [I think to myself] but no one in their right mind would actually take on all that I have on my plate at any given moment. As time flies by, I increasingly worry that I am losing a bit of myself with each passing day.

This is the way it is with Impressive Women. We like looking Impressive... let's face it; it *looks* impressive to do all that we do! We like the sense of accomplishment and the responsibility that comes along with the tasks that we complete each day–on time and within budget–but every now and then, things happen that are out of our control and we lose our ability to get it all done. Then we feel like all eyes are on us because how could we, the Impressive Women, mess things up? So, we don't tell anyone. We get sick instead because that's what "normal" people do. They get the flu and stay home from work and no one bats an eye because it's *normal*. Now, for the Impressive Woman to take a sick day, she has to be practically admitted to the hospital, but *that's what it takes* to get us to stop being so impressive. You see, we often forget to take care of ourselves and, in an effort to please and astound our admirers, we keep saying "Yes" to everyone without considering that we may have already reached the saturation point on our day timers.

Have no fear, dear ones, my recovery time is astonishing. Always the overachiever, you can count on me! When I crash, I crash hard; I am forced to stop everything. In record time, I regroup and I'm back at it again. I use my downtime wisely: I reflect, critique my choices, and vow to make wiser ones in the future. I go through the required self-loathing but ultimately, thriving on the possibility of even more achievement in the coming days, I determinedly get back on the "impressive train" until the next crash. Gosh, I really need to find a way *off* this track. It's killing me.

What if they knew that I am overwhelmed?

I am Lonely

It may seem strange to know that an Impressive Woman like me ever gets lonely. I am surrounded by clients, colleagues, friends and family, almost constantly, in fact. But there have been times in my life when I have suffered the most debilitating loneliness. It feels like a hole in my heart that may never be filled. It is a sense of emptiness that is all-consuming. It feels like despair; the kind of sadness that you would never wish on your worst enemy.

As a single parent sharing joint custody with my ex-husband, I have missed seeing my kids on a daily basis and often feel lonely at night when, after work and the odd television show, I come across a toy or a commercial that makes me think of how empty my life can seem without them. My heart aches when I think of the times that I don't talk to them after school to hear how their day was spent. I worry about missing important milestones as I travel.

Travelling has afforded me the opportunity to make friends throughout the country and, since being divorced, my social life has expanded and I have met some wonderful people. I have discovered that quantity, however, doesn't always equal quality and over the years, I have found myself spending weekends by myself because I have no friends who share a similar interest in the greater pleasures in life. I had friends who served a particular purpose (the movie date, the wine taster, the dancer, the scrap booker) but never any who connected on a deeper level. I have been lonely for a multifaceted friendship so much so that it became one of my New Year's resolutions of past: to attract a number of solid friendships that fulfilled me emotionally, socially, and intellectually.

It is strange to feel alone in a crowd. I have walked into a room, not knowing anyone and wondered, *What if they knew...?* I have thought to myself, "Why am I here? Why would any of these people want to speak to me tonight when they seem to be doing just fine without me?" Some times that sense of loneliness is strong enough for me to turn and walk away, feigning a stomach ache like a young child in the event that someone corners me at the coat check on the way out and asks me why I am leaving.

It may seem natural to feel lonely when you are single. When your mind wanders to all the things that couples do; you yearn for someone to spend long evenings with, cuddled up by a fire with a glass of wine, or someone to walk with through the aisles of Home Depot on a Saturday, picking out paint and wallpaper. Yes, I have felt lonely because I haven't had a man in my life with whom to share my spare time. And sometimes, that loneliness has left me downright miserable.

However, I have also felt loneliness within a relationship. I think that is one of the hardest things that I have experienced. Being in a romantic relationship, yet feeling like your thoughts and feelings do not matter enough to someone to warrant an introduction to his friends and family, or the time to return a phone call, or show up on time for a reservation. When you look with yearning across the living room and get nothing in return, that is a feeling of loneliness–coupled with helplessness–which leaves a lump in your throat and a stone in the pit of your stomach. It is that sense of loneliness that provides the wake-up call: *I would rather be alone than feel lonely*. But that is how I feel.

What if they knew I am lonely?

I am Sad

I can make a long-distance relationship work like nobody's business. It really is the best of both worlds, in my opinion. When we are together, our attention is completely on one another and we take advantage of every moment to make special memories. When we are together, we have fun, talk for hours, lay quietly, get things done. It really is a wonderful way to enjoy each other's company.

And then there's the time that we are apart. Fuelled by the urge to get as much accomplished as possible before my next visit, I am extremely focused and productive during my alone time. I am an Impressive Woman and I use this time to my advantage. We don't talk very often but when we do, there's so much to share that the energy is electric and it's like we are in the same room. I feel like he is there watching over me, in spirit, helping me make decisions that are the best for us.

You see, I am hoping that we will eventually be together... all the time. I haven't quite figured out how that is going to happen but I do know it for certain because—if the truth be told—I can't handle the sadness that accompanies the long-distance relationship. You may be confused because of how this confession started. What I've said above is also the truth.

There is one time in particular that the sadness overwhelms me and I know I cannot withstand it indefinitely. The last day we are together brings such sadness that I can barely function. I do my best to contain it—after all, I don't want to ruin our final hours together—so usually, I putter along and spontaneously emit sobs every now and then. It's not pretty, but what can I do? I've tried going for a walk, taking a shower, and napping. I've tried to work, exercise, and eat. No matter what I do, however, I can't let go of the sadness and I find myself crying uncontrollably, even if it's just for a minute.

I suppose I could allow myself the time to cry until I can't cry anymore. Has anyone ever done that? Does it work? I think I'd be afraid that I'd never recover—that it would be too much for me, emotionally. What if I came undone? Could someone be hospitalized because they were sad? I suppose. I don't want to risk it, however, so I'll swallow half of the tears and get through the last day as best as I can. Maybe that's why I always feel like I gain weight on my trips.

At least my hubby understands. While he tells me, "No crying, now," I'm sure that he'd be more concerned if I wasn't upset about leaving him and getting back to my 'normal' life without him. He knows he is special and that it leaves a hole in my heart every time we part. And just in case I've done too good of a job hiding my tears on the last day (you know, by crying into a towel in the bathroom with the fan on or while cutting up onions), I make sure there are ample waterworks at the airport. Once, I was in such a state that a security officer passed me a box of tissues as I emptied the contents of my laptop bag onto the belt. The funny thing is, *he* always gets to see me this way, but his counterpart in my hometown airport thinks I'm an Impressive Woman!

What if they knew that I am sad?

I am Depressed

When my marriage fell apart, I felt like I was sinking in a rabbit hole that grew deeper and darker every day. I felt like my reason for being had vanished and I could find no motivation to get out of bed. I had no purpose without love in my heart. I had also lost my identity. I didn't know who I was anymore.

For years I had always been part of a couple. *We* even had a nickname because we were always together, seemingly happy. My husband, Neil, and I had become known in our circle of friends as Daneil... that's how everyone had been referring to us for years. We were rarely seen apart; we even work in the same office. Without my 'other half' nothing seemed right. I certainly didn't feel whole. And I felt inadequate, unable to make a valuable contribution at home or at work.

In order to avoid the questions and concern, I hid this from my friends and family. I put on a brave face at the very few gatherings that I attended. At work, I tried my best to fly under the radar. I'd greet everyone in the office, exchange pleasantries, but it was all I could do to not burst into tears each day in my cubicle. So I avoided the lunch room. I no longer loitered around the water cooler to discuss my plans for the weekend or the next vacation. I couldn't bare the possibility of someone's innocent mention of Neil's name. I simply put my head down and plugged away until the clock turned 5:00.

On the surface, I still looked like an Impressive Woman. I heard others say, "It's amazing how she soldiers on, with that brave face. She's handling it all so well." What they don't know is that I'm off to the drugstore to refill my anti-depressant prescription.

I am considering quitting my job. I am considering moving. And, I am considering driving off a cliff on the way home.

As I drive, I remember the good times that are now lost forever. I remember all the broken promises that we had made to be true to each other and to remain committed in good times and bad. My mind replays the last few bitter conversations that we had just before he filed for divorce. How had it come to this? Why wasn't I good enough for him? Maybe if I had tried harder... I should have saved more and spent less; I should have joined the gym and worked harder to lose that last 10 pounds; I should have supported his desire to change careers, but we had so much debt, I just didn't know how we'd cope.

Ironically, I now owe even more money, I am more out of shape than I have ever been, and I eat my way through a bag of Lays every night. While he is painting the town red with a new woman every weekend, I stay at home, and don't intend on going out again. The thought of dating makes me want to throw up. *Who would want me? I am damaged goods.* I can't imagine how I would ever keep the attention of a man I hardly know if I couldn't keep the attention of a man I had known all my adult life. I don't know why anyone would ever want to hang out with me. Neil said I was no fun anymore and that all I ever did was worry about money. I am so afraid of falling in love and having my heart torn out that I'd rather not take the chance. I could never handle the humiliation of being dumped again. And, if he cheated on me, I would die. I'm practically dead now so it wouldn't take much to push me over the edge.

What if they knew I am depressed?

I am Afraid

In most areas of my life, as an Impressive Woman, I am fearless. I take calculated risks and I have benefited from that approach with career success and a solid reputation for making good things happen. But in my relationships with men, I have not experienced lasting happiness. I have not experienced the same risk-reward benefits because my tolerance is extremely low. Why? Because, when it comes to men, I am plagued by fear.

I am afraid he won't notice me. In the beginning, it's all about securing the date. I take incredible pains to present myself to him in the most favourable light so that he will take notice of the Impressive Woman that I am. From my clothes to my hair, the way I laugh at his jokes or point out how much we have in common, I am deliberate in everything I say and do with the end in mind: leave him wanting more!

I am afraid he's noticing everyone else. Now that we've been dating a while, my jealous side sneaks in and messes with my mind. I wonder what he thinks of the girl in accounting with whom he works so closely. When he makes comments about women he sees in passing, I think to myself, "What can I do to avert his attention where it belongs: on me?" I get lost in the obsession to ensure I am the only one he can possibly consider being with... for the rest of our lives!

I'm afraid he'll leave. Now that I have him all to myself, I'm afraid that if I do or say the wrong thing, at any time, he'll bolt. Whenever we fight, I figure it will be the last time I'll see him. I fear he will abandon me because I am not good enough. *Maybe if*

I just try harder or love him more or give him space... whatever it takes, I will do it so that he never thinks of leaving me.

I'm afraid he'll never leave. Sometimes, I wish he would. It is nerve-racking to be in a relationship when, every day, you are consumed with how to please the other person. There never seems to be a moment when I can just enjoy him and he can enjoy me. We are always playing a game and I am growing tired of it. When things get really bad, I wish he'd "man up" and get the hell out. Honestly.

I'm afraid of leaving. I think, ultimately, it will be me that makes the decision to end this relationship. After all, he's getting what he wants all the time. How could I have ever thought he'd leave me? I've been the perfect girlfriend. I am always compromising and giving in to his every whim. If he won't go, it will be left to me to be the bad one. *What will happen to me?*

I'm afraid of being alone. They say 'the devil you know is better than the devil you don't know' and I don't know what life will be like without him. I love being part of a couple. I hate lonely nights at home in front the television watching "Say Yes to the Dress", being reminded of my dreams for a happily-ever-after that have once again been dashed as another relationship ends. As afraid as I am of being alone for the rest of my life, I am more afraid of the consequences if I stay.

I'm afraid that other people will know. My image as an Impressive Woman is at risk if I share my story but, perhaps, it will help someone else who struggles in relationships just like I do.

What if they knew I am afraid?

I am Worried

Late at night, I toss and turn. I can't sleep. I start on my back and take a few deep breaths. After several minutes of staring at the ceiling, I reach for my eye mask. It has helped in the past. *Maybe this will be a good night,* I pray. But, no. I roll to my right and stare at my partner's back, listening to his gentle snoring. I smile and then I instantly hate him because he is asleep and I am not! I resist the urge to wake him up, and roll to the other side. I fluff my pillow. I do all of these things, almost every night. The routine doesn't change; the results don't change; my thoughts don't change. I am consumed with worry.

This has been going on for a while and I have even considered seeking professional advice. What would I tell my doctor? He knows me as the Impressive Wanda. I'm never sick. I visit him only for my annual check up and if the kids come down with a bug. He knows how well I am doing professionally. He likes and respects me.

What if he knew I was worried? I worry about my family and our future. I worry about our money, health, and retirement. I worry about the state of education and health care in our country and our political system that seems so flawed. I worry about the security of our future and the happiness of our grandchildren that haven't even been born. And, I worry about so much more. "No wonder," he'll say, "that you can't get any sleep, Wanda." How would I explain to him that every time I close my eyes, I feel impending doom about the future? But I'm fine when I am awake.

You see, when I am working or socializing with my friends, taking care of my family or weeding the garden, I am okay. My life is quite fulfilling. I am happy with the life that I have created. I am an Impressive Woman with a great marriage, happy children, healthy parents and a terrific group of friends. I love my home; it is beautiful and full of wonderful things that my husband has bought for us. He works hard to provide for our family. Come to think of it, that may be part of the problem. It may seem silly but I admit that I am quite worried that someday, it will all be taken away from me. I'm not sure how. Perhaps my husband will leave me for another woman. Perhaps the house will burn down. Perhaps, after the children move away, I'll turn into a bitter woman who has no career to fill her meaningless days. Perhaps, I'll get sick. There are so many possible ways that I could lose this glorious life that I have. I am amazed that my luck hasn't run out.

When I have coffee with my girlfriends, we are never far into the gossip before someone brings us up to date on the latest drama. There's always a divorce or a bout of cancer wrecking the lives of an acquaintance or family member. Every now and then, we hear about a bankruptcy. Really, there is no shortage of calamities that could take all of my happiness away. I am reminded constantly by my friends, family, and the daily news. I can't escape the reality that disaster could be just around the corner.

What can I do? Perhaps I should stay awake tonight. Just in case...

What if they knew I am worried?

I am Lazy

To be called lazy by my hard-working parents was the biggest insult they could bestow. My parents believed that if you had two legs and two hands, you should *always* be doing something productive. Their idea of "productive" may be different than yours and mine, but as long as you were moving and/or learning, you had no fear of being called lazy.

There were many times, growing up, that I felt like having a lazy day. I'd try to hide away to do nothing, but that voice in my head calling me *Lazy Linda* would make me feel so bad that I'd fill my Sundays reorganizing my bedroom (moving) or writing out lyrics to songs I had taped from the Top 40 (learning). As I got older, friends would want to hang out–doing nothing–at the mall, arcade, or park. As much as I wanted to go, I couldn't get past the fear of disappointing my parents or worse, bringing *shame* upon them if someone saw me! Every now and then, the prodding from my pals broke me and I had to indulge in the laziness. I really liked it!

I had many, many days where I longed to be lazy–I just didn't *want* to use my body or my brain. The notion of not having to be accountable to produce something or achieve a measure of work in an afternoon was so liberating. I felt like even though the world was full of possibility, it didn't matter if I chose to pursue anything or not. I felt so great about being lazy that I really felt like I was *doing* something! The sense of accomplishment that came from doing nothing, lead me to harbour a secret passion for laziness. It has been a life-long secret.

The funny thing is that, years later, I still feel an incredible amount of guilt when my parents call on a Sunday and I am in my pajamas, watching TV, and eating popcorn at three in the afternoon. This doesn't happen very often because I am an Impressive Woman with lots to keep me busy and *productive*; however, I do admit to loving these wonderful days of sloth. Do I confess that I am being lazy? No! Yet I wonder... *Is it possible that they are having a lazy day, too, or that they long to feel that sense of freedom that comes from doing nothing?* It is possible, but not likely. And if they are, they definitely wouldn't admit it! They care more about what other people think than I do. Where do you think I learned it?

What if they knew I am lazy?

I am Bored

I sit on the living room floor with my 9-month-old daughter and let out a sigh. The poor thing doesn't realize what a breath of fresh air she has brought into my life. I don't want to burden her. Thank goodness she is too young to understand, but I tell her my story anyway, just to get it off my chest.

"My darling," I begin, "I am experiencing something that I would never wish for you. Promise me that you won't make the same choices that I have. Please say that you will always follow your heart. Dream big! Don't wait for someone else to rescue you. Don't put all your hopes for happiness in someone else's hands. Don't ever feel that you are not capable of creating your own. You have everything you need inside of you to create a magical life. You are a princess. You deserve the best in life. Go out there and make it happen!

I am so ashamed to tell you that your mother is bored. I am bored with the life that surrounds me. I am bored with the routine. I am bored with the furniture. I feel suffocated by the nothingness that fills each day. I do not make a contribution to the greater world. Everything I do is contained in this home which I now loathe with every fibre of my being.

It wasn't always this way. I used to have a spark that could light up the darkest night. When I walked into a room, people noticed me. I was an Impressive Woman. The funny thing is, some people still think that I am. They don't know the truth. Beyond the iron gates of our private driveway, there is a woman who is dying of boredom. Those gates are like a prison door to me. It amazes me that people find them esthetically pleasing when I want to vomit every time I drive through them. You see, I have a longing to be part of a community that makes a difference. I want to find my purpose in life beyond looking good and buying nice things. I am ashamed that I was temporarily distracted by this shallow life. Where did my drive go? When did I give up?

It is sad to have wasted a life like mine. I wish I could be the Impressive Woman that I used to be. I want to be an example for you, sweet child. You are the blessing in my world. Perhaps, together, we can move forward, into the light. Will you come with me?"

She smiled at me and promised not to reveal my secret. I promised to let it go, some day.

What if they knew I am bored?

I am Selfish

My father was right. I'll give him that. I am selfish. I always have been but I have denied it. I had myself convinced that I was anything but selfish because, as an Impressive Woman, I have created a life that appears as though I am benevolent and altruistic.

I volunteer and attend charity events. I donate my time and money to worthy causes. I am the first to sign up for the office fundraiser each year, and I normally win the prize for the highest number of pledges. It appears to everyone that I am generous and giving but I confess that I have an ulterior motive.

Behind all of the acts of kindness is a hidden agenda. I yearn to be recognized for the contributions I am making. I do this for the attention. I love the accolades. It makes me feel great.

I remember the first time that I experienced it. I was in high school and had just been awarded a scholarship for the volunteer work I had been doing afterschool to tutor younger children. The principal went on and on about how I tirelessly helped others and how I was a fine example of peer mentorship. I couldn't disagree. Those were the facts. But, admittedly, I was in it for the cash. While the tutoring position was voluntary, I knew that no one else in the school was applying for the scholarship, and by spending three afternoons a week doing simple math exercises, I could get myself some easy money.

That day, I received another award that was priceless. My father, the one who always told me I was selfish, whispered into my ear, "I am proud of you." It was the first time that I had ever heard such words from him. He wasn't a mean man, but he was quite emotionally reserved and I had been trying my best for years to impress him enough that he would finally let me know that I was good enough.

In search of a pat on the back, I will do just about anything for anybody. Some people may think this is selfish but, I figure, at least someone else is getting helped along the way. Is that so bad?

When you are single, you are a target. People automatically assume you are selfish because you haven't settled down with a man or started a family. But what's the rush? In fact, where's the appeal? I know so many Impressive Women who have lost all their spark and enthusiasm *since* getting married. Oh sure, they were all excited during the dating years and then the planning of the wedding took over their lives. That, to me, was a sure sign that they were doomed. Why would I give up my independence and my money when I can live how I want now without having to answer to anyone? Do you know how much it costs to raise a family? Do you know how many vacations I can take for the cost of private school tuition? *No, thanks*. I'll take my pay cheque and decide what to do with it and I will be laughing all the way to the bank. This is the dream and I am living it. I wonder if my father is still proud of me. I'm sure he'll never tell. He is selfish, too.

What if they knew I am selfish?

I am Heart-Broken

I am experiencing a weird sensation: there is emptiness inside me but, at the same time, there is aching that is very real. I am wandering around the house aimlessly, from room to room, wringing my hands, taking deep breaths to stifle the sobs that sneak out of me every now and then.

This all started because of miscommunication, as most relationships breakdowns do. Men and women are from different planets; we do not communicate in the same manner and we usually do not understand one another at all. I get it. And I really thought that I had figured out a way around it. *If only I responded with love to every situation; if only I left my ego at the door whenever we were together; if only I...* Yes, I tried. The fact is that I am sad because I didn't always respond in love. Fear, worry, and anxiety have all found a place in my psyche and now we are in the midst of this breakdown with no sign of it being rectified. The love in my heart seems to have evaporated and there is nothing but sadness in its place.

One of the reasons I am sad is that I blame myself for making the same mistakes that I always have when it comes to relationships. I am rendered helpless now. There is nothing I can do to make the hurt go away. There is nothing I can say. It is done and I must face the consequences.

Time heals all wounds, they say. My question is: *How much time?* Each minute that I am heart-broken only seems to bring me further despair. I get overwhelmed with the emotion; I cannot function. To make a cup of tea takes all my ambition. *What has happened to me?*

I am an Impressive Woman. How can it be that I can turn to mush just because another relationship is down the tubes? You'd think that I would have developed tougher skin by now. Perhaps that's just it. The outside of me is tougher; I can paint my face and put on a pretty dress and play the role of an Impressive Woman when everyone is watching. The inside of me, however, is another story completely. Inside, I am soft and tender; I am broken beyond repair.

What if they knew I am heart-broken?

I am Emotional

There are days when I can't stop crying. On those periodic trips to the washrooms to blow my nose and splash cold water on my face, I barely recognize the puffy, glassy eyes staring back at me. *Who is this walking train wreck?* She doesn't look much like an Impressive Woman.

I can be set off by a sad song on the radio, a story about a dying puppy dog, or a greeting card. Once the floodgates are open, however, it can take hours to recover. My emotional state seems so fragile and this is NOT the image I wish to project. So I hide. On days like these, I will do my best to cocoon until my equilibrium returns. I may eat ice cream, snuggle in a blanket, and drink tea. We all have our standard feel-good remedies and they work for a while.

I've tried to track my emotional roller coaster because I am certain there is a pattern. As an Impressive Woman, it makes sense to me to manage this weakness that I have and create a plan to mitigate the risk of being found out. There may be some connection to my hormones; perhaps I'm going through the change of life. I mean, I am almost 50, but I haven't had any other physical symptoms, other than the bulging red eyes that come from a whole evening of tears shed while watching the news. But I track away.

I track my eating; perhaps there is a common preservative that sends me running for the Kleenex or a stimulant that is responsible for creating this emotional alter-ego of mine. I track my menstrual cycle–yes I still have one–and wonder if my hormones are to blame. I also track alcohol consumption, times with friends, and time alone to see if any of these factors are influencing my mood.

Yes, I track away. To this point, however, with evidence mounting in several color-coded journals, I have resigned myself to the fact that my emotions are *no longer in my control.* As an Impressive Woman, this is so hard to admit. I am used to being in control of everything. This is unchartered territory, folks. I really don't know what has become of the person I used to be.

So, if you do happen to see me with the sniffles, please don't ask me what's wrong. Please don't ask me if there's anything you can do. Please walk slowly away, do not judge me, and remember that I'm an Impressive Woman who is trying to make sense of it all, and make a come-back!

What if they knew I am emotional?

I am a Bitch

I may as well confess. When something happens that rubs me the wrong way, I can be downright bitchy. I can cut someone in two with a word or even a look. There will be no doubt in the mind of the person who says the wrong thing to me that they have ruffled my feathers, and now have to pay the price.

Usually, I'm quite content to put down my head and work away at my projects whether I am at home or at work. I like to do things at my own pace, without the input of other people. I have experienced a lot of success doing things like this, so why would I change? I think if there was a poll taken in my office about my personality, the *last* thing anyone would say is that I am a bitch. I get along well with everyone, always have a smile, and even bring in coffee to the team once a week. I think people would call me dedicated, hardworking, and focused. A few unlucky colleagues may have experienced my wrath over the years but I think that they know better than to expose me in a survey. Really, it doesn't happen that often and when it does—believe me—it is warranted.

You see, every now and then, when the pressure mounts because of a tight deadline or an irate customer, my tolerance drops significantly and my inner bitch kicks in to overdrive. When my work is negatively impacted by another's lack of dedication, hard work or focus, I am not impressed. My mission to fix whatever someone else screwed up takes over my mind and body and you can be guaranteed that it will be fixed. If anyone crosses my path while I'm on this mission, they had better give me a wide berth or step up to help!

It usually starts with muttering under my breath. I let out a few good sighs and roll my eyes if someone asks me, "How's it going?" I like to rip up paper; it gives me a good release and doesn't create much of a commotion. But when the perpetrator slinks into my cubicle looking all apologetic and fails to offer assistance, I cannot help but let him or her have a piece of my mind. I feel disrespected when the mistakes of one person create additional work for me. I already have enough to do. Why would I want to stay late to clean up this mess? We may be human, but there are reasonable expectations to place on those who hold critical roles in the company. *Am I wrong?* No. And I let them know it. The next day, when the problem is solved, I am fine again. I have returned to my post as the Impressive Woman of the office and there are no hard feelings. Let us hope there isn't a next time!

What if they knew I am a bitch?

I am Old

I feel like I am fighting a genetic war against wrinkles, cellulite, and hammertoes. Gravity has become my worst enemy. If I was a man, I'd probably been worrying about baldness, too. But alas, my hair worries have been limited to the cost of perms and straighteners, chemicals and products, and more electric devices and ozone-depleting sprays; balding may actually be a blessing.

Each morning I wake up, I say a little prayer of thanks that I am still on this side of the ground, and then my work begins! There's a lot involved with maintaining a youthful appearance when it seems that the Universe has other intentions! I am usually satisfied with the end result: my face painted, grey hairs carefully hidden and coloured ones sprayed into place, and nicely fitting clothes that are age-appropriate (for someone 10 years younger).

But then, I hit the big bad world and everywhere I go, I am reminded that I am old! Remember when coffee was just coffee? It came in a bottle and you scooped it out with a spoon. Now, I have to pay almost $5 in order to get my "grande no-foam skinny mocha latte". When did things get so complicated? Going through the drive-thru at Starbucks adds 10 minutes to my drive in the morning but it gives me a break from the traffic which has become horrendous. The road I take to the office used to be two lanes. Now it is four, in most parts; but don't forget the ramps and overpasses, turning lanes and traffic lights to accommodate the new subdivisions. My morning commute can take up to 45-minutes now when it used to take 15! All this complaining makes me feel old. Ug.

By the time I get into work, the caffeine has kicked in—thank goodness—and I am ready to make things happen. Alas, I am surrounded with Gen Ys who spend more time around the water cooler talking about reality shows than they do working. Honestly, I just don't understand the younger generation at work. What happened to the values of hard work? There was a time when you were lucky to have a job. But try telling this to them... I recommend against it, actually.

I was talking about hockey the other day with a 22-year-old. If that wasn't unusual enough, the conversation began because he didn't understand why most 'old' people either cheered for Montreal or Toronto when there are so many other choices. So I told him that, *back in the day*, we only had two channels on our television set and CBC only carried the games from the east. I don't think he quite understood. I think that he thought I didn't know what I was talking about because I appear to be much younger than I really am! This conversation proved to him that I was a dinosaur, even though I am technically *young* enough to be his mother.

What if they knew I am old?

I am a Nag

I just don't understand why people don't do what they say they are going to do unless I nag them to death! In order to get anything accomplished that involves other people, I have to constantly remind them what needs to be done, how, and when. Seriously, if I could do everything myself, I would. At least then, I'd know what to expect.

It's true that I have become a nag just like my grandmother! Oh, the stories my father used to tell me and the bits that I witnessed myself. The family talked about how she would be forever picking on them. The way I see it, however, is that my grandmother wanted her household to run efficiently. She was the CEO of her home but couldn't do everything herself so she relied on her husband and four boys to help out. *Is this so wrong?* Why are we ridiculed for insisting that people pull their weight and deliver with excellence? At home or work, it doesn't matter... nagging is necessary if you strive for perfection in a world where so many accept mediocrity.

Honestly, I do get tired of it. I really wish that I could spend more time working on my own stuff instead of checking that of others. I wish I could trust people. It's really like a compulsion. Maybe it's genetic (I love you, Nan!). As soon as I ask someone to do something, I put a reminder in my own calendar to follow up. Will I ever be rid of this inner-nag that has taken over so much of my personality? Seriously, when I plan my week ahead, the day-timer is riddled with notations to check in.

- **School projects.** Are they up to date? Do we need to shop for supplies? Is there a permission slip or money owing for that? When is it due?
- **Friday night with the girls.** Who is bringing what to the potluck? Who will be designated driver? Does everyone have a babysitter? Is my good dress back from the drycleaner?
- **Date night with hubby.** What are we going to do? Did he make reservations? Are we meeting anyone? Are the kids' sleepovers arranged?
- **Work.** Where do all the departments sit on budgets and timelines? Who called in sick today? Do we have someone to cover the phones at lunch time? Is the photocopier working? Have invitations to the trade show been sent?
- **Home.** Has everyone sorted their laundry and put it in the baskets? Is there anything special you want in your lunch boxes this week? Tuesday is grocery day. Don't forget to put out the garbage and change the kitty litter.
- **Personal.** When will I schedule my hair and nail appointments? What three days will I go to the gym? I need to remember to schedule some quiet time for myself–I need to get that novel read!

As you can see, it is a demanding life and I have to keep on top of it so it runs smoothly. One false move, and the whole thing could come crashing down! [I even nag myself as you can see from the last bullet point.]

As an Impressive Woman, I recognize that much of my success has come because I have worked well with other people but sometimes I fear that the nagging has me pegged as a bitch. I really try to do it nicely but, *come on!* When you've been reminded electronically, in print, by phone, and in person and you still fail to perform, what do you expect? So, yes, I can be a nag. But I get results and, in the end, that's what counts. The other thing is that, with the exception of a few close work colleagues and family members, nobody knows this side of me. They only see the results and that is how I'm judged. So, I'll continue to hold on to this aspect of me because it serves me well (and because it connects me to my Nan). I just won't publicize it while I reap the benefits that outweigh the costs.

What if they knew I am a nag?

I am a Shopaholic

STACEY, 27

I bought a new dress today. It felt fantastic! I love the feeling of hanging something wonderful in my closet. It brings me more pleasure than actually wearing it. It's strange but true. The thrill of buying a new purse or pair of shoes is quite remarkable; so much so, that I usually shop for myself at least once per pay period. I like to think of shopping as a reward for the contribution that I make at work every day. Actually, my shopping is a contribution of another kind... to the economy! I am proud to say that I do my fair share in both cases.

It's hard to say *when* I prefer to shop but I can break it down into several categories:

When I am in need. This is the most utilitarian and least rewarding. Underwear, milk, facial cleanser. Check, check, check. Yep, this is my least favorite reason to shop. I'm in and out so quick it makes the greeters at Walmart spin. That's, of course, because I know exactly where everything is on the shelves in every aisle. I'm there so often, I should get commission on what I buy! Really, I know half the staff.

Following a break-up. This is classic retail therapy here, folks. I haven't had the need for this type of shopping in a while, but you know what I mean, don't you? When you have no one to cuddle up next to on the sofa, why not drown your sorrows in a new cashmere sweater, a comfy pair of slippers, a soft pastel throw, and a bottle of merlot? Perhaps your style is a new yoga outfit from lululemon AND a gigantic tub of Haagen-Dazs. It doesn't matter. You are hurting and giving yourself a present goes a long way to making you feel a lot better. Let's face it: you'll probably buy yourself something much nicer than HE ever did... the jerk! PS–A longer relationship warrants much more intense therapy... perhaps a new couch and matching wing back chair OR a trip to Hawaii.

Girls Night Out. Oh yeah! It's pay day and we're off to celebrate with our hard-earned cash in hand. Dinner, drinks, shopping, and a chick flick to round out the night. We may actually take in a matinee, then shop, eat, and drink. It all depends on the mood. Whatever the schedule, one thing is guaranteed: shopping with my gal-pals is intensely fun! We buy make-up, hair accessories, shoes, purses, and clothes for our men. There is no rule about how much we spend or who buys how much; however, we make a rule NOT to go into dressing rooms. We've been there, done that, and almost got kicked out of the mall for having *too much* fun. Imagine!

Marathon outlet shopping. Once each year, the ladies in my family hop a plane with two empty suitcases each. That's right– empty. We take a change of undies in our purses, just in case of an unexpected delay, but otherwise, we allow maximum space for our purchases. We are like seasoned professionals. *[Wouldn't it be amazing to be paid to do this???]* We get the hotel shuttle to the outlet mall, synchronize our watches and agree to reconvene in three hours. It sounds a little crazy, but we do pace ourselves. And, we have a plan. Each of us has a specialty and we trust one another to actually shop *for* us! It has worked really well, allowing the greatest distance covered in the least amount of time. We limit ourselves to three hours in the morning. We break for lunch and have a dip in the pool in the early afternoon. By 3:00, we are back again for the final items to be crossed off our lists. Generally, we take two days to fill our suitcases. We shop together for shoes and lingerie because it is much more difficult to delegate and a lot of fun since we have different tastes! After all the damage to the credit cards, not to mention the exchange rate and the duty, you'd think we wouldn't shop again for another year, but...

Special occasions. I love to shop for other people so when I've got the excuse of a special occasion, it's "no holds barred" for this shopping diva! I have tried to work with a list. I have tried to work with a budget. But, honestly, I like to let the wind blow me where it may. I am a free-spirited shopper. I love to be inspired as I walk the aisles of my favourite department stores. I get goose bumps when I see the divine sweater for my mother on display in a shop window downtown. Those kiosks in the mall make me squeal with delight with the make-up and jewellery that is simply sensational for my girlfriends. And, don't get me started on the number of yummy pullovers I have bought for my beloved. He is so handsome that everything I buy looks great on him! Let the shopping goddesses shine down on this Impressive Woman. Lead me to the perfect gift every time. I am in my bliss!

What if they knew I am a shopaholic?

I am Trapped

For the past several years—10, in fact—I have felt like I was a prisoner in someone else's body. More accurately, I have felt trapped in a life that I designed when I was blindfolded. You see, I willingly participated in every decision that has shaped my current reality; however, the clarity that has come from self-inquiry has led me to believe that I must suffer from deep self-loathing to have built a life that doesn't serve to make me happy.

How is this possible? From the outside, my life looks quite wonderful. I am the Impressive Woman who has the luxury of staying home, a committed long-term relationship, two growing children, friends and family nearby. *Who wouldn't want this life?* Well... me.

I must take responsibility. I created this mess. Now I can't get out of it. I gave up my career and now I have no experience. I quit university to follow my husband and now I don't have the education either. I don't have an income to support myself. If I leave what kind of job will I get? What kind of income can I earn? How will I ever support myself and my children? Why did I do this to myself?

And why does everyone think I'm so impressive? Sure I go to the PTA meetings, bake cookies, host elaborate parties, keep my garden pristine, and have the best decorated house on the block at Christmastime. What they don't know is that I would walk away from it all in a minute because it doesn't fulfill me. I feel suffocated. I feel like a princess trapped in a tower waiting to be rescued.

But I don't want another man to whom I am in debt. I need to break free without the aid of a man. *But how?*

Gosh, I feel so trapped! My mind is going in circles coming up with different options, but ultimately, they all lead to dead ends. I cannot see my way out of this situation. Perhaps I'll start squirreling away some money, without my husband knowing. Perhaps I'll take an on-line course and get a certification in pet-grooming. Perhaps I'll just bide my time until the children are out on their own and then I'll run away. In my fantasies, I am the cruise director on the Love Boat. *I wonder if I could do that?* An Impressive Woman can dream. No one can take that away from me and it's one thing that I haven't given up.

What if they knew I am trapped?

I am Desperate

There is a sense of urgency in my thoughts. I need to make things happen now. I am desperate for the success that eludes me. Yes, I *appear* as though I am successful; I am an Impressive Woman who has accomplished much in these 38 years. However, there is more on the horizon; I can feel it.

There is a greatness that awaits me and I'm not interested in taking the scenic route. I want to get there now. I want to experience all the good that is coming to me. I have earned it. To this end, each day, I pray in desperation for the way to be revealed. My prayers are usually silent but today, I am intent on getting the answers I seek, so I pray out loud:

"Please, please, please. Let today be the day that my dreams come true. I have been an Impressive Woman. I have worked hard. I have been a good wife and mother. I volunteer. I contribute. Please don't let any more time go by before I realize the dreams that I have put on hold for so long. I am ready. Can't you see that? Please, please, please. I am desperate."

What do I want so desperately? Well, it's kind of hard to explain but I want to feel like I am part of something *bigger*. Over the years, as I have been busy doing everything I was expected to do, I lost my own sense of purpose. I have been going through the motions of life on autopilot for so long that I can barely remember where I want to go. Lately, I have been receiving flashes of insight that remind me of the dreams that were once very important to me. It's hard to believe that so many years have passed without having them come true. I have certainly achieved many other milestones in my life and I have been happy along the way as my

86

career and family life flourished. But I now feel an overwhelming desire to put myself first and get moving on a whole new path.

I have always been a fairly intense person. When I focus on a goal, there's not much that stops me. That is why I have become somewhat frustrated with this process because it isn't happening fast enough. *What do I need to do to change the course of my life?* I desperately need to make a connection with a higher purpose. I feel like I have a calling that has gone unfulfilled and the sense that I am meant to do more has created a hole that I cannot wait to fill. "Help me! I feel like I am drowning!"

What if they knew that I am desperate?

I am Weak

"Do not tempt me with that chocolate!" Why is it that when you make a declaration, the Universe tests you right away? Have you ever noticed that? It happens to me all the time. As an Impressive Woman, I am prone to making commitments; it's practically an addiction. I commit to more stuff on a daily basis than most people do in a month, I am sure.

At work, these commitments are easy enough to keep. I run from meeting to meeting, always on time, doing my part to make a valued contribution to the greater vision. At home, I keep my promises to chauffeur the kids, pick up the dry cleaning, and prepare everyone's favorite meals. My friends know they can count on me to show up on time and bring the good wine, always full of stories and laughter.

So what's the problem? The problem is that I can't seem to keep commitments I make to myself. Whether I commit to going to the gym three times a week, giving up chocolate for Lent, or treating myself to a movie, I always find an excuse to renege. As an Impressive Woman, my plate is constantly full of things to do. I don't stop from the time I wake up in the morning to the time I fall in bed at night. I am always doing, doing, doing. Rare is the time when I take a breather and do something just for me. I recognize that this is a pattern of mine and that it really isn't healthy. So I beat myself up a bit and then make another promise to take better care of myself. And, then, out comes the chocolate!!

I am weak. I feel so bad when I break my promises. The hit to my self-esteem is tremendous. It makes me want to eat even more chocolate! When I sense the weakness coming on, I allow it to take over my body. I succumb to the urge to do what I know is "wrong" and feel the temporary "good". *Who doesn't feel good after eating chocolate, really?* But then the betrayal kicks in and I begin to feel the hurt that I would never intentionally inflict on anyone. I acknowledge that I would *never* let another person down like that; I would *never* break a promise or make someone do something that is clearly not in his or her best interest; I would *never* encourage or support choices that are obviously destructive. *Why do I do this to myself?*

It is always *after* the betrayal that I can become the observer and truly see what I am doing to myself. The insight is humbling: this is an act of self-sabotage because of some deep sense that I am less deserving of integrity than others. I'm still working on this character flaw but for now, I'll recommit to making healthy choices that serve me and loving myself unconditionally. If only I could get to this point of knowing *before* eating the chocolate. One day...

What if they knew I am weak?

I am a Smoker

I confess. I have been a closet smoker for about 30 years. I have, quite literally smoked in closets so that no one would know of this bad habit of mine. I graduated to the cellar, the garage, and even a broken down tree house in the woods behind my home, but I choose to enjoy my smokes in solitude, always.

It started when I was 10. I decided to try out these long Benson and Hedges cigarettes that my mother smoked so elegantly. I was in awe of how she made the smoke quickly go out of her mouth and up her nose and then slowly let it billow out. It was majestic; a real art. Of course, it took many years of a scattered puff and cough here and there to figure out that inhaling a cigarette was really a science and definitely, at times, anything but elegant. With true diligence, however, I was up for the challenge and by the time I was in high school I could hold my own. My witness: the mirror.

Since I couldn't safely smoke in the closet, I took to finding places with a little more elbow room and a handy-dandy mirror so I could observe my progress as I attempted to blow smoke rings and get that smoke curling just right. I was quite enamoured of myself as I smoked. I thought I looked very glamorous. But yet, I knew that I would be keeping this secret for a long time because good girls (later to become Impressive Women) just don't smoke.

In my late teens I finally let down my guard in front of my best friend. It turned out that she had been smoking in the closet, too! Oh, what freedom we experienced when our parents went away for the evening or we babysat together for chain-smoking social climbers who always had stacks of "rollies" (and plenty of mirrors) in their dens. I would always come home reeking of tobacco but it was easy enough to explain away. After all, back then, smokers could light up everywhere!

Times have changed and smoking has become quite taboo. There have been occasions when I have given up the cloak and dagger bit and smoked out in the open. This has happened only when I travel and usually out of the country. I remember thinking, *"Is there anything sweeter?"* as I sat on a balcony in Cuba, puffing away, drinking rum, and reading a trashy novel. We do get such pleasure from the "forbidden".

Alas, back home, faced with another Canadian winter, I kick the habit for the cold months. It just isn't logical to stand outdoors in the snow to light one up so... I wait. Quitting has really never been difficult for me. I used to do it whenever I was around people, after all. And, one of these days, I'm sure I will quit for good.

What if they knew I am a smoker?

I am Nervous

I have a nervous habit. It's an odd thing that I do whenever I am worried about the immediate future. The funny thing is that I'm not always conscious that I am nervous, until I feel the familiar unpleasantness that comes from biting my nails to the quick.

Since I was little, I have chewed my nails. It has turned into a compulsion that catches me off guard and by surprise when I realize I am doing it. *How can I not be aware that I am eating a piece of my own body?* How gross, right? I figure that I am so ashamed of this disgusting habit that I even block it from my conscious self.

It's really not the kind of thing you'd expect an Impressive Woman to be doing. I know I'm not all that old but isn't biting nails a phase you go through when you are, like, five or something? It makes sense that you'd pick it up after thumb-sucking gets boring, but shouldn't you give it up by the time you hit Kindergarten? Well, I never did. Back then, I would do my best to hide the damage with cool bandages (on the worst fingers—there were always two that were so bad they'd bleed). Most of my schoolmates didn't even notice but I would be uber-embarrassed whenever I'd have to point out a spot on the globe or use finger paint (with only 8 fingers) because that would draw attention to my nasty habit.

As I got older, I continued with my secret habit—always in private. I guess that's when I had more time to think (and worry). When I was busy at school or with friends, I was usually having fun and didn't feel the urge to mutilate my body. When I was alone, however, my nails became my pastime. I was either picking, chewing, or painting them. By the time I was in high school, the camouflage had changed from bandages to nail polish. It never once dawned on me that bright pink polish might actually bring more attention to me—but what can I say, I like pink!

Now, because of my nervous habit, I'd be lucky if I made it through a couple of days without destroying my beautifully painted nails. *Did I ever go through the nail polish remover! Let me tell you.* The smell of acetone in the house would be strong enough to burn your nose hairs! Unfortunately, I was undeterred. I used my babysitting money to cover the cost of bottle after bottle of polish and remover. While my friends spent hours chatting on-line, I used the excuse that my parents wouldn't allow me; the truth was that my fingertips often hurt too much to type. And, of course, I needed to allow time for my nails to dry on grooming nights!

Yes, this habit of mine has interfered with my life, it's true. I also think that the fear that someone would find out about the compulsion has left me paranoid and somewhat deceitful. *How did it come to this?* Isn't it bad enough that I feel worried about things that I don't even know I'm worried about and that I mutilate my own body? Why do I have to carry the guilt about a nervous habit that I just can't control?

What if they knew I am nervous?

I am Stubborn

I love astrology. I love to use astrology to explain away a variety of phenomenon. I particularly love to use astrology to explain away my various character flaws. As a Taurus who also happens to be born under the North Node of Pisces and in the Chinese Year of the Dog, I am the proud recipient of a triple dose of the stubborn trait. What that means is that *Being Right* was divinely bestowed upon me and that conceding would simply be in violation of cosmic laws that are quite a lot greater than me or you, thank you very much.

When you and I enter into a conversation where we hold different opinions, you may as well know from the start that I am stubborn. Since I was "born this way" you really don't have much hope of persuading me to see your side or that of any other person, for that matter. I am set on being right and I will go to the grave with that attitude. Yes, it *may* just kill me, but I will die proving myself right!

I think my stubbornness, masking as "tenacious" and "determined" is why many people see me as an Impressive Woman. They know that, as the company spokesperson, I am unwavering in my stance. I will never back down and I will always stand up for what I believe in. When I approach my boss for additional funding for a new project, my staff can be assured that I will prevail; I prepare myself with the appropriate company vernacular and tell the boss what he wants to hear, but since I know I am right, that confidence (once again, nicely masking the arrogance that is the best buddy of stubbornness) carries me to victory every time. It's not just me that benefits from this bull-headedness as you can see.

94

If you've got it in your sights to challenge me, however, you had better be prepared to "get the horns"!

I am unyielding when I know I am right. I can be downright rude, if the truth be told. I am not always proud of how I behave but when I am right, I think, "Why should I step aside to save face?" And another good question is: "Why should I be the one to concede?" If we are talking about giving people the benefit of the doubt or just "agreeing to disagree" (what kind of pansy saying is that, anyway?), then why do *I* have to be the one to do it? It's just not my style. I am a Taurus, after all!

What if they knew I am stubborn?

I am Tired

Do you have any idea how much energy it takes to be an Impressive Woman? Seriously, I don't know how I do it. I wear many hats and my responsibilities keep me running from 6:00AM to midnight every day of the week. I never slow down—even to a comfortable pace—for fear of what might not get done. The truth is I am so tired I could fall asleep at a moment's notice; anywhere, anytime.

When I say I am tired, I do mean that my body feels like it isn't getting enough rest. How can it? Six hours a day just doesn't cut it yet it is the only "down time" I get; I am always going from place to place, barely taking a pee-break throughout the day. [That's a bit of an exaggeration because I *schedule* washroom breaks every three hours, so my bladder doesn't collect any unwanted bacteria. I definitely do *not* have time for a late-night trip to the emergency room for antibiotics.] The notion of taking a coffee break at work or eating lunch away from my desk is a joke. There is always so much to do that I can't afford the distraction. If, for some strange reason, my inbox is actually empty, there are countless personal things I can do while my colleagues sit around discussing the latest reality TV show. What a waste of time that is!

When I say I am tired I also mean that I am tired of living this way. It is exhausting to manage everything all the time. Of course, the fact that I hold extremely high standards for myself doesn't help matters. In fact, I realize that my perfectionism actually adds to the burdens I carry. I acknowledge that I take much more time to do tasks because I need all aspects to be "just right". Whether I am cleaning the house, doing my taxes, or polishing the car, I will work painstakingly hard to ensure it meets my gold standard.

I am an Impressive Woman with a reputation and I do not want anyone to know that I try so hard and that all of this business makes me so tired!

What a dream it would be to have some time to myself–quiet time, when I could kick back and relax. In this dream I would sip tea and read a novel [I used to *love* reading], curled up in my big leather arm chair that never gets used. I would play soft music in the background and, every now and then, I'd get up and do those yoga poses that I've always wanted to try. That dream of mine would have me rested and re-energized so that I could *be* more and *do* more and *have* more... hmm... perhaps there is some logic to this dream after all.

But wait! It's 5:00PM and that little daydream cost me three minutes of productivity! I have to stay a bit later at the office now and then I'll get tied up in traffic and the kids will be upset that I didn't pick them up on time and then I'll buy fast food to make it up to them and hate myself afterward because of the unhealthy choice; while helping the kids with homework, I'll do laundry, vacuum, and make lunches for tomorrow just before I fall into bed thinking how nice it would be if I could just read a novel. One last thought: I don't think I can do it anymore. *ZZZzzzzzzz*

What if they knew I am tired?

I am Hurt

Have you ever been betrayed by a best friend and felt the sting of hurt at the mention of her name? I have. I am still reeling from the devastation. It has been several months since I learned that my confidant and bosom buddy decided to cut me out of her life.

In case you are wondering how this could happen without my knowledge or participation, I want to clarify: *she* made this decision without discussing it with me. Six years of friendship was flushed down the toilet. [An offensive statement, yes, but appropriate, as I consider now that she was *full of crap* when she told me during our last visit how much she cherished our friendship and that I had brought so much joy into her life that she didn't know how she could ever repay me.] I really had no inkling that there were any issues between us. We had gotten along famously since our initial introduction. We talked several times a week and saw each other most weekends. Our husbands and children were also friends, which makes this situation even more difficult. Her decision has hurt more than just me, but I appear to be taking it the hardest.

I have lost my best friend and I am going through a period of grieving; I think I'm actually in the fourth stage now: depression. First, I was in denial. When she didn't return my calls, I excused it away. When weeks passed without an invitation to a movie or Sunday brunch, I figured she must be working a lot of overtime shifts. But when my 40th birthday came and went without presents from her or her presence, I quickly moved into stage number two: anger. *Who did she think she was to unilaterally end our friendship? Did she think I was just going to sit by and allow this to happen?* I was mad at her for abandoning me! In stage three, I looked pathetic:

I left messages—to no avail—begging her to meet with me. I kept thinking, "If only I had the chance to talk to her, we could work this out." The rejection I experienced, coupled with the hurt, has left me squarely depressed.

I look forward to the day when I can finally move into acceptance and learn to trust again. In addition to losing that friend, I also lost a tremendous amount of faith in people; it has been quite the blow. Intellectually, I realize how important it is, as an Impressive Woman, to develop strong relationships with others in order to succeed in life, but emotionally, this loss has really taken its toll and I will need significant time to heal.

What if they knew I am hurt?

I am Sorry

There comes a time in everyone's life when you recognize that you haven't always made the best choices. At one point in time, you hurt someone; that may have been someone you love. You may have also been hurt yourself, but you come to realize that, until you apologize, that hurt will never go away.

I have decided that the time has come for me to step up, with an open heart, and take responsibility for the hurt that I have caused. It will be nice to think of that person without the guilt that I have been carrying for years. I have known for a long time that I should say, "I am sorry." Now I can have a clear conscience because I have done all I could possibly do in that relationship to heal it and to honour it. *Instantly, I feel different!* I feel like I have healed something deep within myself, even though I am the one apologizing. I wonder if it's possible that the other person will respond in kind. I guess it is possible; however, that is not the point of this exercise.

These three words are seldom used when we are too busy being right and proving others wrong. I realize now that these three words can mean all the difference in the world and everyone is just waiting for you to step up and be brave enough to say them. I am glad to do that today. I am no longer willing to let time pass without making amends. Relationships are too important. Love is what makes the world go around but that won't happen until I walk through my fear of rejection and tell people how I truly feel.

There are many people to whom I am sorry. I am sorry for the ways that I have acted, the lies I have told, and the tricks that

I have played. I am sorry for cheating, hiding, and playing small. I am sorry I didn't do more or that I did too much. I am sorry that I was wrong about you. I am sorry that I was right. Most of all, I am sorry that our relationship ended and I didn't apologize sooner. An Impressive Woman isn't worried about saving face. An Impressive Woman has the courage to do what must be done to make things right with other people because she recognizes their value and appreciates the gift that each one brings.

While this is a blanket apology to everyone that has ever touched my life, I trust you will accept it with the open and loving heart that I know you have. I wish you the best in everything. I am blessed to have had you in my life. Thank you.

What if they knew I am sorry?

I am a Victim

All my life, it seems, I have been marching to the beat of someone else's drum. If I was told to jump, I'd ask, "How high?" I wasn't concerned with how safe it was, whether it was a good idea, or how it might affect my sense of self, my finances, or my health. I just went ahead and jumped because it would please and that, I felt, was my purpose: to please.

While it always seems like a good idea to please others, the truth is revealed in how you feel after the fact. I don't usually feel good. To tell the truth, the general sense I have is that I am a victim.

These days, I don't often feel like I am doing things out of the goodness of my heart. While I am an Impressive Woman and I am a kind and generous person, I feel like I have fallen into a pattern of doing things just to "keep the peace". I feel like people take advantage of me. I feel manipulated and used. Have you ever felt this way? How does it make you feel? It makes me feel dirty. And, what I've noticed of late is that *everyone* does this to me!

My kids. I swear they think I am their servant. From the time I get up, I am picking up their clothes, searching for books, packing lunches, signing permissions slips, driving them somewhere, and giving them money. Do they ever stop to ask what my plans are? Do they ever wonder how I do all that I do? Do they ever thank me? I don't think so.

My friends. Why am I always the one who has to plan everything? Why do I have to call everyone for the movies, organize the potluck, and send the reading list out for the book club? Why can't anyone else do it? I imagine a time when I can just "show up" and have no responsibility except to have a good time. I wonder if they know how much I feel burdened that the success of every get-together rests on my shoulders. I'm really tired of it.

My parents. I feel obligated to spend every Sunday with my parents. Why? Because they invite me and I just can't decline. They are lonely, I think, and they need me. But, when I arrive, we don't ever have pleasant conversation. They don't ask how I am. The conversation is always about the children and all that I am doing wrong when it comes to being a working mother. Whenever they call me throughout the week, I am inundated with, "What are you doing about *this*? What are you doing about *that*?" It's exhausting! I feel so belittled after our visits and calls that, sometimes, I wish I didn't have to talk to them at all. And then I feel ashamed. The cycle of victimhood continues. I'm guessing that I actually learned it from my parents.

My husband. And then there's the man who promised to love me for better or worse. I wonder if he'd love me if I didn't do whatever he asked. I suppose I've never given him the chance. To be fair, I made it my mission, when we got married, to be the source of his happiness forever. I didn't realize that doing so would eventually wear me down because what made him happy didn't necessarily make me happy. I gave up on my dreams to help him pursue his. At first, I thought this would be a temporary situation–that the pendulum would eventually swing my way–but 15 years later, I'm still waiting. And, damn, I am resentful!

My boss. As an Impressive Woman, I walk into work each day ready to give my all. I am there to serve my boss and serve him I do. I answer all his questions, prepare his correspondence, and file all his paperwork. I practically run that office for him. But where has it gotten me? He won't promote me because I'm "too valuable". Yeah, I'm so valuable that I didn't get a raise this year! I wonder if there's some way I can work on commission.

Perhaps I can get paid for every time I say, "Yes, Sir," without wincing in pain.

I wonder what would happen if I just said, "No!" I'd probably spend the next month in the hospital because of all the heart attacks I'd cause. But I'll never know. This is a pattern of behaviour that I can't imagine breaking. While it doesn't serve me, it does make everyone else happy. And that's why I do what I do.

What if they knew I am a victim?

I am Looking for Attention

Why else would I write a book? I am looking for attention. Fame and fortune are coming my way. WooHoo! That's right, baby. It's all about me!

A while back, in a coffee shop, I was told by a close friend that she no longer wanted to be in my life. She thought I had changed and I was no longer who I had appeared to be. She believed that my motives were no longer in alignment with her values and she was protecting herself by cutting ties with me. She felt that I had become completely self-centered and by choosing to be a coach, speaker and author, I was only looking to make money from other people's misfortune. *Ouch!*

I could have countered her remarks in many ways: with sarcasm, indignation, self-deprecating humour, humility, or sheepishness. The fact was that I was so shocked that my friend felt this way, that I was rendered speechless... for a few minutes. Then, the realization kicked in that we were in a public place and other people might hear what she was saying. I felt embarrassed and humiliated but she didn't appear to notice (or didn't care—she was on a roll). I actually raised my hand as I got up from the table and calmly said, "Please stop. Enough." I hung my head low and walked my red face out of that coffee shop, all the while wondering, *Is she right? Had I turned to the dark side? Was I just another user of people? Is that what my motives have been all along and I've actually been defrauding people with a motivational mask?* I wasn't sure.

She wasn't the first person to question my motives, although she was the one who knew me best. I'm not sure why people doubt the intentions of others when they try to do good; I suppose everyone has their own reasons for not trusting. It has stung when people have asked, *"You do that for a living?"* or *"You get paid to motivate people?"* Maybe it stung because there was a part of me that couldn't believe it either. Here I am, living the dream. I am doing what I always wanted to do. I have taken risks and they are paying off with a new life that is grounded in my personal values. My journey has been full of twists and turns, and I keep learning valuable lessons at every pit stop. That day in the coffee shop was no different.

For the rest of the afternoon, I thought about the things she had said. I knew I was in danger of slipping into a rabbit hole because of this feedback. *How could she doubt my motives? Hadn't I been a wonderful friend to her? Hadn't she been promoting my work to everyone she knew?* I had trained myself to "be the observer of my life" without losing myself in the process, and that's what I needed to do. I allowed myself a few hours of quiet contemplation to receive insight and dispose of this issue once and for all.

While this may not be all there is to it, here's what I discovered that day:

There is an aspect of my personality that always looks for attention. I have sought the limelight since I was little, from school plays to social committees. I have worked hard and I have enjoyed the recognition. I admit to liking it when people openly acknowledge my contribution. To her point, I believe there is a self-centeredness that exists and a desire for approval that hasn't been "cured" with age. Another thing that I haven't grown out of is my desire to help others.

Ever since I was little, I have lived in possibility. I am the one who sees the potential in every situation and in every body. This optimism (some would call it idealism) has provided me with a good life as I have attracted a fair degree of success, both personally and professionally. But, this trait of mine has also caused me, and other people, significant grief; of that, am I not proud. I could beat myself up about the mistakes I have made, but to what end? Every choice I have made has brought me to this point, and I am very happy where I am. I am proud of the life that I have created and I am excited to be on this journey, living with deliberate intent as an Impressive Woman.

As an Impressive Woman, I have learned that when you step out of the pack to lead, you provide the opportunity for people to point their fingers at you–in pride or in envy–and I have experienced both throughout my 41 years. It doesn't feel comfortable to be singled out for success *or* failure but that's the position you are in when you decide to "play a big game". I feel secure that I always try my best and, for the most part, my intentions are quite pure. If someone questions that, I do not take it personally. As Mother Teresa put it so eloquently, "In the final analysis, it is between you and God. It was never between you and them anyway."

Sadly, there are people who question my motives, but I don't blame them. You see, my friend is an Impressive Woman, just like me. She has many traits that are to be admired. She also has aspects of her personality that she has been hiding for years. I believe, that on that fateful day, she revealed one of those to me, and I forgive her for that. I trust that she will forgive my frailties as well and come to value me for the contribution I am.

This is my wish for us all. BE worthy of admiration. BE there for your family, your friends, your community, and yourself. BE the centre of your own universe. Stand in your power like I am standing in mine. BE in awe of yourself. BE an Impressive Woman! Move through your life with grace, confidence, and excitement.

What if they knew I am looking for attention?

Part Two

I Have Courage

It takes a lot of guts to start your life over at, what used to be known as, "middle age". But that's exactly what have I decided to do. After my marriage of 12 years ended, I look upon the clean slate that is my future and get very excited. Well, I *was* scared to death... but only momentarily; the opportunity to tap into the reserve of courage that had been growing for 36 years is now upon me and I intend to follow through.

It is like walking up to the edge of a cliff. I can see that what lies beyond the next step is full of possibility. It is beautiful and holds so much promise for an Impressive Woman like me. I am inspired by all that I can be beyond the next step. I am euphoric. I am poised at an empty canvas and I am the artist. Recreating my life is going to be the most fulfilling "challenge" that I will ever accept.

I know that, in order to taste the sweet nectar of success, I will have to summon every ounce of courage in my heart and soul. I teeter on the edge for a little while but the anticipation soon wins me over. Happiness eluded me in my "old" life and the opportunity to start over is right in front of me. How can I *not* go for it?

I could allow my fear to stop me but then I wouldn't be honouring the Impressive Woman that I know myself to be. I have fought a hard internal battle along my journey and I am proud to say that I have (not only survived, but) thrived since I have reclaimed my power. *What have I got to lose?* The probability that I will succeed is quite high—after all, I am an Impressive Woman.

With a clear sense of who I am and the willingness to accept myself fully, I move confidently into the unknown. The only thing that would make this adventure sweeter is if there was a bunch of other Impressive Women standing on the ledge with me so that, without parachutes, we could take the great big leap into our brilliant futures together. Come along with me! Here I go...!

What if they knew I have courage?

I am Honest

There comes a point in every Impressive Woman's life when she must face facts. I came to that point a couple of months ago when things weren't working for me in a few areas of my life. I found that I was always playing the "blame game" and was increasingly unhappy with my outer world. My health, relationships, finances and career were all suffering and I kept looking outside of myself to find out why. One day, I came across an interesting quote of Confucius that gave me the perspective I needed: "No matter where you go, there you are."

I had been hiding from the truth in this magical land where I was always right and everyone else around me was to blame for my misfortunes. There was no shortage of people who were affecting my ability to live a happy, fulfilling life. But when I started to see that I was the common denominator in each of the problem scenarios, I realized that the blame lay squarely on my shoulders. If I wanted to create a life that was truly reflective of the Impressive Woman that I was, I had to take responsibility for the energy I was putting out and the choices I was making every day. I accepted that, in order to be satisfied with my life, I would have to first get really honest about what was happening and what contribution I was making. Only after I accepted responsibility for the choices that I had made to produce my current reality, would I be free to create something new and wonderful in each area of my life.

Health. I started with my health. I had been in denial that my health was pretty good. While I saw the doctor annually for my

113

pelvic exam and to get my cholesterol and blood pressure checked, I wasn't doing anything else to proactively manage my health. I was getting older but hadn't adapted my health regimen to reflect the needs of a 45-year-old. If I was to be completely honest, my eating and exercising habits had gone down the tubes when I accepted a promotion at work. I worked through lunch most days, stopped going to the gym after the office closed, and often got takeout on the way home. I blamed my new work situation on my lack of discipline. That excuse served me for five years! Rather, it didn't serve me at all. When I got honest with myself, I saw that my habits were sabotaging my desire to lead a healthy lifestyle. I had the power to change.

Relationships. With great trepidation, I sat down one night with a journal to record all the things I liked and didn't like about each of the most important relationships in my life: my boyfriend, my parents, my boss, and my best friend. I was a little scared at what I would reveal because some of the relationships had been on shaky ground as of late. I wrote for two hours! When it was done, I noticed a lot of patterns. I also realized that there were a lot more positive aspects of my relationships than I had been recognizing. I had been focusing too much energy on minor issues when, really, I was fortunate to have attracted wonderful people into my life. I congratulated myself on being the kind of person that people wanted to be around AND I decided to begin anew and honour those relationships from a place of gratitude and respect. When I was honest, I realized *I* hadn't always acted as the girlfriend, daughter, employee, or friend that I wanted to be. I wanted to be better. I knew that the success of those relationships was in my hands and I needed to change how I was being.

Finances. It had been years since I sat down with my investment advisor and it was time to get really clear about my financial situation. I had simply been filing the monthly statements that I'd get in the mail because I didn't want to know what was happening with my retirement fund. I made an appointment and allowed him to lay it all out for me. We made a new household budget to reflect changes in my income and spending habits so that it was realistic and meaningful. I set savings goals and recommitted to paying down debt and building my nest egg. I was relieved to learn that my finances weren't nearly as bad as I was making them out to be AND I felt a renewed sense of control over that part of my life.

By being honest with myself and taking responsibility for the reality that I was experiencing, I moved into a place of acceptance. From there, I could clearly see that I had been living like a victim and not at all as the Impressive Woman that I am. Amazing!

What if they knew I am honest?

I Have Faith

Let go and let God, they say, in practically every self-help book I have ever read. As an Impressive Woman who likes to be in control of everything, that is easier said than done. *Are you with me?*

As the years have passed, however, I have discovered that when I hold on too tight to the things (or people) I love, my need to control usually results in disaster. It took a long time for me to learn this lesson, and it was very painful at points, but I have learned it finally. I have learned the lesson that success comes with surrender and with the faith that everything is as it should be.

There is a part of me that has always believed that things happen for a reason. I believe in synchronicity. I am not superstitious but when a name comes into my consciousness three times in a row, I act! Each time I have done this, I have been rewarded with miracles small and large. When I have demonstrated faith that there is a force greater than myself that knows best, I have been aptly rewarded in ways that are immeasurable but ways that have brought me significant joy that is only possible when you are connected to your Higher Self.

In order to access this faith, I have learned to "get out of my head". Again, for a type A, over-achieving doer that this Impressive Woman has always been, it was one of the most challenging lessons of my life. When I've been faced with problems in the past, I switch very quickly into problem solving mode and don't allow much room in my brain for insight as, I am certain, that I have the answer if I just work at it hard and long enough. *Does this sound familiar to you?*

In recent years, I opened myself up to the possibility that I actually do not have all the answers—in my head, anyway. I believe that I do have *access* to all the answers but as long as my mind is running 100 miles an hour, there is no opportunity for the insight to present itself. There are a few techniques that I have learned to calm my mind, get me out of that frenzied problem solving space, and open to receive inspired solutions.

- **Bubble baths.** I used to say that I never had time for baths but once I discovered their healing power, I was hooked. Slipping into the tub cleanses the body and the mind from all the toxic energy that you've attracted throughout the day. The silence and soothing calm of the water provides a peaceful haven to let go and allow inspired solutions to come to mind.
- **Meditation.** Beginning my day with 10 minutes of meditation has changed my life. I usually sit up cross-legged and visualize the different colors of my chakras but, in the beginning, I used to listen to a myriad of guided mediations which helped me focus on setting intentions for the day, one of which is always to be open to receive divine guidance. This practice has grounded me and provides a sense of connection with my Higher Self that can easily get lost when I am busy.
- **Count to 10.** For times when life gets "out of control" and my mind finds its way back to the familiar chaos, I simply remember to count to 10. It seems juvenile (so juvenile that most people don't do it) but like most things we learn in childhood, it really does work! I close my office door and blinds, go into a bathroom stall, close my eyes at the traffic lights—it doesn't matter where you do this—and listen to myself breathe for 10 seconds. When you listen to your breath, you

come into the present moment. There are no problems in the present moment, only your breath. *Hello!* You've just provided yourself with enough time for divine insight.

It took me a long time to learn to have faith in my ability to receive the solutions to my problems. If I had learned this lesson before, it would have saved me years of frustration and heartaches. I would have likely had fewer wrinkles and grey hair, too. But, I guess that is all part of a bigger plan. At least, that is what I have come to believe.

What if they knew I have faith?

I am Confident

Today, I start a new job. I decided to switch careers because my former work environment was not in alignment with my values. Specifically, I was expected to work long hours and travel each month and that took me away from my young family more than I liked. While the salary and benefits were quite attractive, my experience with this particular employer left me feeling undervalued and disrespected and I finally found the courage to leave. As I grew very clear about what was important to me as an Impressive Woman, my confidence in myself grew and I was no longer willing to accept a career that did not reflect my values.

When I first graduated from university, I thought that getting a job *anywhere* was something to celebrate. The job market was not all that healthy and the stories that I heard from other people in my field led me to believe that any job that paid the bills would be a sensible choice. Back in the day, I was a fairly confident individual. Despite what my colleagues shared, I held the ideal that I would work for a company whose work I supported and whose culture I fit. I was successful in securing an entry level management position at an established firm in my home town and I was confident that my star was on the rise.

I worked hard and reaped the rewards. The company spent a great deal of time and effort to engage and retain its top talent and they benefitted from increased loyalty in return. My confidence in myself as a productive member of the team was never in question. I knew where I stood and I was proud of my accomplishments. But things at home weren't going as well and there came a point that my confidence in my performance as a wife and mother was deteriorating rapidly and I needed to be thrown a life vest in order to save myself and my family.

That life vest came, ironically, at a management retreat that was hosted by my employer. As a participant, I had to evaluate my life against my personal values. This was one of the most challenging things I had ever been asked to do. I had forgotten what was important to me as I flew through every day trying my best to be there for everyone else—my boss, my coworkers, my clients, and my family. I came to the realizations that I had been regularly neglecting my family ever since I got a promotion at work a year ago.

Like any Impressive Woman, however, I was up for the challenge in front of me and I dove head-on into the task of rediscovering my core values as instructed. In twenty minutes, this exercise provided the wake-up call that I desperately needed to turn my life around. I was shocked at the plain truth that was staring up at me from the worksheet: my life did not reflect my values. No wonder I was feeling disconnecting and unfulfilled.

In that moment, I chose to make a change. I chose to honour my values and to set about creating a new life for me and my family. I didn't know, at that time, that it would mean I would have to leave my job, but I was willing to make that change if necessary. I had confidence in myself as an Impressive Woman to do what needed to be done. I took responsibility for the choices I had made and for the opportunity to make it better. What a difference it has made!

What if they knew I am confident?

I am Free

I sit on the couch on a Monday evening in July and bask in the warm sun rays that seep through the living room window. I am in my glee. I am almost overwhelmed with giddiness that is hard to contain. I laugh out loud and shake a little. I even say to myself, "Can you believe it? You are free!"

Freedom, sweet freedom. I don't think it can really be appreciated unless you have experienced a life without it. Imagine living your life however you want, without the expectations of others to influence your decisions. Imagine going where you want, when you want, and with whom you want, without having to check if it's to the approval of someone else. Imagine choosing what to wear or what to eat or what to say based on your own self of sense, instead of asking for validation from your partner, friend or parent.

I gained this freedom recently and what occurred to me is that I never have to let it go again! Why would I? This feels so awesome!

For a long time I lived as a martyr. I have come to terms with my choices and have owned up to my part in creating the unhappy circumstances that filled my life. With freedom and independence grasped firmly in my hand, I have had twinges of concern that I might be too afraid to open myself up to relationships ever again for fear of falling back into the same trap as before. I suppose that is a valid concern but I haven't worked this hard to move out of a fear-based lifestyle to take a new one. Instead, I choose to be grateful in every moment for my freedom and to celebrate by believing with all my heart and soul that it is possible to have freedom *within* a relationship.

I believe that within a healthy, interdependent relationship, romantic or not, both parties can be free to act or speak without restraint which is congruent with the definition I found on-line of "freedom". I believe that a relationship demands respect, but that this respect is not an obligation but a choice, and therefore does not exist to restrict freedom. Respect is giving mutually and as a fundamental component of the relationship. When respect is present, as a (love-based as opposed to fear-based) response, and both parties accept all that they are–individually and within the relationship–they can be truly free. And as George Michael sang, "I don't belong to you and you don't belong to me." Imagine how powerful two people can be in such a relationship!

Thinking back to that mystical Monday evening, I believe now that it was the realization–that I fully accepted myself for who I am–that made me giddy. I am so proud of myself for reclaiming my freedom and my power!

What if they knew I am free?

I am Resilient

From one angle, it looks like my life has been plagued by one disaster after another. Why is that I don't look at it that way? Sure, I've always been a positive person but when you've got evidence that is unquestionable, why wouldn't you agree that life has been harsh? Am I simply in denial? Am I going through life wearing rose-colored glasses? Am I being honest with myself when I say that my life has had its challenges but that I haven't found a challenge yet that I haven't overcome?

I don't consider myself to be any more special than the next person. I don't believe that I am deserving of more or less fortune or disaster. When something bad happens, I never respond, "Why me?" because that would inherently mean that I think someone else might be more deserving and that's just not true!

But, in order to humour you, I will list a number of things that have happened to me over the past 10 years, since I turned legal drinking age in Canada (seems like a good place to start and you'll see why).

- Alcohol poisoning at my first big college party
- Charged with plagiarism (and later exonerated)
- Fired from summer job
- Sexually harassed during my first week in my job
- Left hanging by disgruntled roommate with 3 months of overdue bills to pay
- Car broken into and CDs stolen
- Hard drive wiped by computer virus
- Spray tan gone very, very bad (I mean ORANGE)

- Root canal
- Broken wedding engagement

I mean, really, some of these things even seem comical to see them in black and white, while they were all painful when I was in the moment. You could call me *Calamity Jane* but I refuse to wear any other label than *Resilient Rhonda*. Yes, I am picking up the pieces again from perhaps the greatest challenge so far: the broken wedding engagement but honestly, I'm enjoying every minute of it! You may think I'm delusional but I consider myself blessed in so many ways and believe that my life has unfolded this way to teach me what I haven't already learned and I am grateful.

I keep saying, "You can't keep an Impressive Woman down." I will keep going, on my journey of success, and will not allow my positive attitude to be swayed by the occasional detour. I will always count my blessings and remember that there are people struggling with much more than has ever been throw my way. If and when the day comes that the Universe decides to knock me down even harder, I believe my resilience will grow in kind to match it and I will prevail!

What if they knew I am resilient?

I am Talented

I excel at everything I try. Of course, I am selective of what I try. As an Impressive Woman, I know my strengths and I use them to my advantage. I like to win; I like to succeed. I do not like disappointment; therefore, I am very calculated when it comes to taking on new challenges. The fact is that I am very talented in certain areas of life.

Organizing an event. I am a chronic list-maker and that comes in handy when I am tasked with organizing. I start from the big picture and work my way down, setting priorities, and establishing deadlines. I also love to delegate but I only do this once the "end in mind" is clear. There is no point sending someone off to buy decorations if they don't understand what the room is supposed to look like in the end, right? I enjoy the process of organizing so much that I am always the first to volunteer at the office or at home to plan and execute the next big event. It is gratifying. It gives me an opportunity to really demonstrate my talent.

Remembering names. It is my party trick. When I leave, I will always go around the room, shaking hands or hugging every person I met that evening, calling them by name. People are amazed that I don't miss a single one. Do I use mnemonic devices or other memory strategies to remember? No. It is a gift that I have always had. I am a "people person", that is for sure. I think it helps to be genuinely interested in getting to know people. When I am introduced to a new person, even in a busy or loud setting, I do my best to focus and retain what I am being told. I will ask questions that reveal something unique about him or her. I think this helps, too, as I not only remember the name but something useful to recall when I see them again or if I decide to follow up with an email. It brings me a lot of joy to remember people's names. I think it makes them feel important; and, they are!

Public speaking. While this is one of the biggest fears of North Americans, I have never had trouble speaking in front of a group. If I am asked at work to deliver a presentation, I jump at the opportunity. It is very rewarding to share information or insight to a group of people, to hold them captive, and influence their decisions. I take this responsibility very seriously and always prepare my material in advance and practice my delivery. Lately, however, as I have grown to accept that public speaking is an innate talent of mine, I have allowed myself to *trust* that everything will be fine and that I can handle whatever the audience throws at me. That adds an element of excitement that I wasn't open to experience before. It's cool. Again, I've excelled every time.

Facilitating meetings. I like to be in charge of the flow of meetings. I am organized and I don't mind leading a group discussion. I am good at it and it frustrates me to attend a meeting that is ineffective. I'm always prepared with an agenda that is distributed ahead of time. People are aware, in advance, of any requirements or expected contribution. I set out the clear intention of the meeting so that everyone knows why it is important that he or she participate. I want everyone to feel that it was worthwhile to attend and that their input was valued. I start and end on time and if additional time is needed to accomplish more, I will involve only those people who are critical to the tasks at hand. I respect the time and talent of my colleagues and I am sure they appreciate it.

What if they knew I am talented?

I am Committed

As I embark on a new beginning, I am reminded that my success is completely dependent on the commitment I am willing to make to myself. Because I am determined to create a new life that is full of happiness and harmony, I promise to honour myself as I would any other person. I make this commitment because I am worthy.

In order to strengthen this commitment, I have written a long story in my journal about why I deserve this new life. I poured out my history of misfortune and mistreatment. I laid out all the ugly details in black and white so that I could see that I had suffered enough. Then I affirmed that I have no further burden to carry. I have no penance to pay. It is my time. I am ready.

I make my commitment meaningful by recording a list of reasons *why* I need to make this change. I consider the implications to my health, my finances, my relationships, and my career if I stay where I am. I think about the person I have been for the past 20 years and who I wish to be going forward. I acknowledge the incredible opportunity that is in front of me to make a difference in the lives of others as I step boldly into a new world.

Based on my history of failed promises to make positive change, I enlisted the help of an accountability partner. I have shared my vision, in its splendid entirety, with my best friend. I have also shared with her the strategies that I intend to implement over the coming 12 months in order to manage the transition and ultimately achieve the one-year goals I have set. I have shared with her the reasons why I am committed to making those changes so that, when I am challenged, she will remind me to stay focused and keep on heading down that path to happiness and harmony.

A vision board is affixed to my bedroom wall now where once there was a wedding picture. It is full of pictures and words that inspire me and keep me emotionally connected to my dream. Whenever I look at it, I smile. I check in with my intentions for the day to ensure they are in alignment with that big picture of happiness and harmony. My commitment is so strong I can feel it in every fibre of my being. I know that I will have everything I desire.

In my bedside table, I have a beautiful journal that I visit every night. I don't always write in it; sometimes, I read what I have written before because it reminds me of how far I have come. When I lose my way, it helps to ground me. I am proud of my progress. I am proud that I stayed true to myself because I am worthy.

What if they knew I am committed?

I am Deliberate

DEBBIE, 44

What power is there in deliberate intent? Perhaps you have born witness to thoughts creating results as I have. I have felt the power that comes from manifesting with intentional thought, but when a loved one faced surgery, I wondered whether I was powerful enough to raise the healing vibration for him on my own. My desire to make a difference was so strong that I decided to enlist a few more bodies for the cause. Indeed, the power of deliberate intent is dramatically magnified when multiplied by hundreds of souls, all sending love and positive energy at the same moment in time, just when it is most needed.

As the date of the surgery neared, I fell into a pattern of negative emotions that is quite commonly experienced by those who have to look on as a loved one is suffering. I felt powerless as I sat at home while my boyfriend was across the country for a week having surgery to remove a tumour. The wave of emotions that were constantly churning kept me distracted, unable to focus at home or at work. The full week seems like a blur. Again, I am sure if you have had a go through a similar experience, you may have felt like this. What I learned upon reflection of the process I went through is this: When we feel there is nothing we can do, no way that we can make an impact, no escape from the fear in our hearts, no turning off the tears—when we find ourselves consumed by our fear-based thoughts—we CAN turn it around.

After I decided that I no longer wished to be consumed by these fear-based emotions and thoughts of helplessness, I took a deep breath (several, actually) and got grounded. I emptied my mind of all the fear, all the uncertainty, and doubt. When I was able to open up my soul, the answers came: when you feel helpless, there IS always something you can do. The answer will always come once you detach from the emotion, still your mind, and open your heart to receive the answers–you already have them within you. When you are in a place where fear resides, you are closed off to the possibilities. You are closed off to love. And love holds all the answers.

A walk in the woods always helps when I need to ground myself. That is how the process often starts for me. This week was no exception. A few quiet moments overlooking the pounding surf and a walk on the tree-lined trail provided me with the clarity I was seeking.

I was gentle with myself as I accepted responsibility for having created the pain I was feeling. Accepting that I could control only one thing in this situation–my response to it–was a great relief. I was not responsible for anything else. I understood that the sense of hopelessness was completely of my own creation and I was ready to let it go. It wasn't serving me or anyone else. I recognized that I was experiencing many of the patterns of thought that have plagued me at other stressful times in my life. I knew that underestimating our strength in tough times, is a trap laid by the Ego. I was not interested in staying in that mindset for long.

I was ready to see what was possible in the situation. I opened myself up to the inspiration I found on that walk in the woods. I saw that my unique gifts could be used to make a contribution to the healing process and I could step up and make a difference. Although I couldn't control the operation, I could not be there to hold his hand, I did believe with all my heart that I had the power within me to raise the healing vibration that could be felt when he needed it the most. Another epiphany: *I did not have to do this alone!* In fact, I planned to engage others to tap into the infinite power of the collective deliberate intent.

With this renewed sense of purpose, I bounded out of the woods, making calls on my Blackberry to people who I could enlist to help me make my vision a reality. Within hours, I had established a facebook group that would call on people to deliberately send their thoughts and prayers of healing energy at the same time.

It was a powerful movement. I believe that this effort created an energetic wave that was not only felt by its intended recipient, but by everyone involved. We were collectively sending love out to the Universe; how could it not be a profound experience? I was embracing my potential from the time I emerged from the woods and as I did, I empowered others to do the same. That is me, living my life on purpose! That was my big lesson learned: when you feel powerless, turn to the power *within*. It is there, just waiting to be released!

What if they knew I am deliberate?

I am Focused

"Laser sharp" is how you would describe me when I am on a mission. It is one of my greatest strengths, I think. As a young Impressive Woman, I have a lot on my plate and I quickly learned that to be successful at wearing many hats, one needs to be fabulously focused. I have honed my skills to the benefit of everyone around me.

I have noticed that, while many women claim they are masters of multi-tasking, they often appear "scattered" and frequently suffer from overwhelm. Perhaps the way they are juggling everything doesn't allow them to be present with any one activity. I think I am more like a man in the way I am able to compartmentalize my tasks and prioritize them based on competing demands of my time, energy and talent. Is it right to believe that it is a more masculine trait to be focused? I'm not sure, but at this young age, I am a sponge and my conclusion is simply based on observation of friends, family and coworkers. I have always been a keen observer and like to analyze what I see and create a way of being for myself that combines the best practices of others.

Planning. I plan everything—even my down time. [If I didn't, I probably wouldn't take any.] At the beginning of each year, I set my goals for the year and each month I do the same. At the beginning of each week, I take out calendar and block out time for all the activities that will help me attain my long- and short-term goals. This way, I never feel guilty that I am taking time away from work, the boyfriend, or myself, because it has all been accounted for in advance. I do leave "wiggle room" for spontaneity but that usually falls on the weekend when I block out time for friends and family. I may not know what I'll be doing with them, but I do know my attention will be only on them and they will appreciate it.

Prioritizing. Setting priorities has helped me greatly when it comes to making the best use of my time, particularly in the workplace. While there are always fires to be put out, I am not responsible for them all. Where possible, I proactively work on the 20 percent that generates 80 percent of the revenue. I plan my workday activities–meetings, paperwork, correspondence, and strategizing–around the team's vision of success. And I encourage everyone around me to do the same so we can support each other in that endeavour.

Efficiency. I try to control my time as best I can, setting myself up to minimize time-wasters and maximize productivity. I have learned how to organize my office for the most efficient handling of emails, reports, and client files. I have found that solid systems work wonders in maintaining control and getting things accomplished in a sensible manner without getting side-tracked or overwhelmed with the sheer volume.

Being present. When I start a project–at home or at work–I dedicated myself to it fully. If I am washing the car, I am washing the car; I'm not watering the plants, chatting with the neighbour, or solving life's problems in my head. If I am hiking with my friends, I am hiking with my friends; I'm not texting my boyfriend, gossiping about people who are not there, or thinking about work. This approach gives me great pleasure as I focus intently on what I am doing; it gives me the freedom to fully enjoy the moment.

Delegating. There are things that I don't like to do. There are also things that other people do much better than I. I don't pretend to be the master of all skills and I am not above asking for help. I *am* about getting things done so I enlist help when I feel that my time, energy and talent could be spent elsewhere, but there are tasks that need the attention of a qualified body and mind. When I delegate, I am always clear about my expectations and I make sure that I express deep gratitude when I ask for someone's help, and when I receive it. To be successful, you have to surround yourself with people who have complementary skills. This is a fantastic piece of wisdom I was glad to learn early in life.

Satisfaction. No matter what task I cross off my to-do list, I take a moment to feel deeply satisfied that I got the job done. I am proud of myself for the way that I manage all my responsibilities. I have developed systems and processes that allow me to capitalize on my strengths and maximize my effectiveness. This has allowed me to experience great success as an Impressive Woman and I intend to celebrate every little win. I highly recommend it!

What if they knew I am focused?

I am Hard-Working

I learned from my parents early on that anything worth doing is worth doing well. I grew up in a home that valued hard work and there was evidence of it all around me. Luckily, it was always a home where play and celebration were equally as important—once the work was done, of course!

As a kid, I was the one who studied for longer hours and took up a paper route to earn my spending money. I understood that my first priority was to do well in school but I wasn't being given a "free ride" at home; no, if I wanted to have money for entertainment or fancy clothes, I'd have to work for it. I didn't resent this attitude because it was the normal conversation in our home. My parents worked in order that we would enjoy a certain standard of living. Why would I be exempt from that way of being?

I did get to enjoy many of the fun things about being a kid: long bike rides on Saturdays, swimming with friends on Sundays, and a trip to the mainland every summer. I think I appreciated my free time much more than other people my age because I felt I had earned it. I didn't feel I was entitled to it. It was a reward because, throughout the week, I made a solid contribution to my family and the community: I helped out around the house; I never missed a day of school; I volunteered at the library; and I delivered the newspaper. Yes, I relished my free time. I was always grateful.

I have never grown out of this sense of responsibility to work hard. You may expect me to say that I work long hours and save all the fun for the weekends or the one trip down south each year, but that's not true. Thanks to my parents, I learned very early that a happy life is a balanced life.

After university, I set out to land myself a good job and I have progressively moved up the corporate ladder over the past 25 years because I have worked hard. When I am at work, I am focused, efficient, and innovative. I never doubt that I am giving it my all and I am proud of all that I have accomplished. But I have always stood my ground to protect my free time. I have communicated it with my employer and I am respected for it. My boss knows that there are few people who are as diligent as me. I get more accomplished in eight hours than many people do in a week so I am never asked to work past 5:00 or on the weekends.

My evenings and weekends are filled with other responsibilities that I take just as seriously as my work. I maintain a lovely home with a husband and three children. We share the chores throughout the week nights and participate in community and school events as a family. My parents live close by and spend a couple of nights each week visiting with us. Weekends have always included quiet time for me as well as fun time with my close friends, doing something active (or sometimes just drinking wine).

This is the life that I chose to create because of the value of hard work that was instilled in me as a child. I wouldn't have it any other way. I am an Impressive Woman who reaps the rewards every day.

What if they knew I am hard-working?

I am Dependable

As a friend or as a co-worker, you can depend on me. I am always there when you need me to pitch in. I have "saved the day" on more than one occasion by bringing an extra dessert to the party or coming up with a brilliant sales pitch to secure a new client. When you here the phase, "I knew I could count on you," chances are, I am the subject of the conversation.

I don't do this for the accolades, however. Please don't think that of me. Please don't get the impression that I sit around waiting for the opportune moment and swoop in to take all the glory for the successful party or meeting. It's not like that at all. I simply try my best to be there for the people in my life who need me.

I have always been fortunate to be surrounded by dependable people. I live to serve and make a difference. When I know that a friend is planning a big celebration, for example, I always offer to help. I know I would appreciate the same if the shoe was on the other foot. I also know how important it is to come through when you promise to help. There is nothing worse than not being able to depend on someone. I have felt such disappointment in the past and I vow to never inflict that on anyone.

It is sad that so few people really act like their word is their bond. I hadn't given it much thought until one particular summer when I was "helping out" more than usual. I had recently changed careers and I had a lot more free time. It was the party season and I accepted at least one invitation each weekend. I was in the habit of saying, "Is there anything I can do?" I really didn't mind. That is how I roll. What amazes me, looking back, is how often I was met with a look of shock or surprise when I actually did what I said

I was going to do. And I did all kinds of things. My dependable self has blown up balloons, picked up dry-cleaning, cooked meals, chauffeured the drunk, babysat the young, chopped vegetables, strung patio lights, baked desserts, and vacuumed floors.

There are not many limitations on what I will do for the people in my life. Do I expect anything in return? No. I also realize that not everyone will reciprocate and that some, who offer, with good intentions, will let me down. It's ok. I don't take it personally. It will not deter me. Being dependable has served me well because I have a life that fulfills me and it is worth every bit of effort.

What if they knew I am dependable?

I am Strong

Let's hear it for Girl Power! That's what I told myself as I shovelled my way out of the driveway this morning in the rain!!! [Yes, where I live, a rainfall after a dump of snow is quite common.] When you're facing Mother Nature's sense of humour, the best defense is a good offense—and that is a *healthier* sense of humour and a lot of strength! I may have missed the garbage truck—since I was getting myself dressed appropriately for shovelling, but I did manage to get it around the corner to the neighbour's house and under his net before anyone could see! Take THAT Garbage Man! (Apparently, I haven't gotten over the time that they refused to take my garbage because it wasn't under a net AND left me a nasty note.)

So with a smile on my face I dug my way out and then felt that familiar sense of satisfaction from being a strong, capable woman. Today I encounter many such women. I salute them and celebrate.

Being a fully self-expressed woman, it is important to show the world your true colors—the feminine, vulnerable side, the caring nurturing side, as well as the confident independent side. Begin strong enough to handle whatever is thrown at you in the run of a very busy day is something this Impressive Woman has embraced and it has made all the difference.

They say what doesn't kill you makes you stronger. Lord knows that I'm as a strong as 50 men! I've endured job loss, sexual harassment, heartbreak, relocation, illness, and the death of a parent. And I'm not dead yet so you know what that means! I am strong. This doesn't mean that I don't cry, because I do. I release the pain, anger, fear, and insecurity that come when you face loss. I have learned that bottling it up inside makes me sick or weak, so to speak. So I honour my feelings and I let them out in healthy ways like journaling, talking with friends, and physical exertion (like shovelling!).

Dealing with my emotions keeps me grounded. I believe that is one of the reasons I am so strong. When I get hit with bad situations, I usually respond in a fairly calm and collected manner. I deal with the facts first. I assess the situation. I try not to place blame or judgment. I simply accept what is. This has helped me tremendously especially when faced with the biggest challenges of my life. I've learned not to take things personally but to learn the lesson and move on. I don't hold grudges. I preserve my energy and that keeps me positive in the face of obstacles.

Obstacles are not going to go away. Show me a life without challenge, and I'll show you a boring and unproductive life. I expect to always have ups and downs because I live like an Impressive Woman. I am fully engaged in my world and love every second of it. Bring it on, I say. I am ready!

What if they knew I am strong?

I am Loving

I never knew what it was to love another human being until my daughter was born. To conceive of this kind of love was not even possible. I had no inkling that it would be like this. As I hold my baby, I am completely in the present moment. I don't remember childbirth; I don't remember the cracked nipples; I don't remember the sleepless nights. All I know is what I feel right now. I love her so deeply it fills every fibre of my being. How lucky am I?

We have our quiet time together now that I am on maternity leave. At first, it was quite an adjustment for me to be home. I had taken a few weeks off before the delivery to prepare for her arrival and I felt anxious about how I would fill my time. Wow! Has my perspective ever changed! I laugh now to think about it because my days are so full. Within a month after she arrived, she and I became quite active and have been fortunate to continue making the most of our time together. We aren't going *all* day, but we do make an effort to get fresh air regularly and some companionship for Mommy who still likes to indulge in some girl talk with friends and browsing the bookstore for a juicy new novel to read during the baby's nap.

Honestly, I admit that my favourite time of the day has now become the (very) early morning feeding when my husband is still asleep and my baby girl and I have a special quiet time in her room. We listen to classic music while I nurse her; I tell her stories while I change her diaper; and, while I rock her back to sleep, I talk to her about how we will spend our day together, being happy and loving.

We make big plans about the future, too, my daughter and I. I share my dreams with her. (She is such a good listener.) I make promises to her to support and nurture her so that she grows to be an Impressive Woman. I want the best for her. I can't imagine anything bad ever happening to her but I will provide her a loving foundation so that she grows confident and capable of managing obstacles without losing herself. I wish, too, that she has the opportunity one day to feel love like this. It is the most remarkable feeling in the world. If I had nothing else, this would make me the most successful woman in the world.

What if they knew I am loving?

I am Joyful

JENNIFER, 31

A wildly popular women's magazine featured a brilliant article with the title, "What makes you smile?" *Why was this so brilliant?* Well, do *you* know what makes *you* smile? I didn't. I had never given it any thought. Sure, I seemed happy enough. I am an Impressive Woman, gaining momentum on my journey of success, driven to accomplish my goals and make other people happy but I still didn't feel confident in answering that question.

Aha! The stark realization emerged as I was reading through the suggested strategies to create a joyful life: I had been living primarily to *achieve*, not to experience. I was always working toward the next big goal. *I'll be successful when...* I can hear myself now. And, further, what I did for "fun" was usually someone else's idea of fun. My time outside of work was full of obligations to other people. I'm not saying that I didn't enjoy them because, most often, I did, to some degree. However, what I am saying, and what this article made crystal clear, was that I was not deliberately filling my life with joy.

So I set out on a mission—to honour the goal-oriented fool that I can be! As I do whenever I am about to step outside my comfort zone and try something new or solve a problem, I made a list. I bought a brand new journal, sat alone in my bedroom, lit a candle, sipped on some wine, and thought, "What makes me smile?"

Let me start with: *a fresh journal, alone time, candles, wine.* Hmm... That was easy! Then the sorry flash of awareness that I couldn't recall the last time I did this. I felt like I was indulging. The guilt of taking time for myself started to come over me, but I stuck to my plan... I was going to complete this list; or, at least, put a good

143

dent into it. So, I gave myself an hour of solitude and here's what I produced:

- Dancing in my kitchen
- Breakfast outdoors
- Singing in the car
- My new leather chair
- Fresh flowers
- Manners
- A quickly returned email
- A well-written book
- Surprises
- Friends over for dinner
- Bright colors
- Watching children play
- Walking on the beach
- My new red shoes

This may not seem like much to you, but I had a major breakthrough that evening and it completely changed the way I looked at life. For everything I wrote on that list (which grew and grew as the days went by), I had a reason that it wasn't something I regularly experienced. While it gave me pleasure, it may have been dependent on the weather or other people, or not having enough time, energy or money. *All crap. All excuses.* I set out to change my experience of life and to surround myself, every day, with things that brought me joy.

I got in the habit of asking myself each morning, "What will bring me joy today?" It might be a hike with a friend, coffee with my mother, or fresh flowers for the dinner table. I might buy myself a new CD, plan a potluck, or take a drive down the coast. Every day was different but every day held the possibility of joy. That is my newfound mission in life. I do this for myself and I do it for the other people in my life. When I'm smiling, I am a much more Impressive Woman and we're all grateful for that!

What if they knew I am joyful?

I am Connected

I used to go through life reacting to whatever was thrown in my direction. I was always moving at such a high velocity that I didn't have time to think about how I was responding or if there might be a better way. Don't get me wrong, I always did my best. I wasn't lazy or non-committal. I am an Impressive Woman, after all. The problem was that I just didn't consider the implications of my decisions and whether or not they served my higher purpose. The fact that I wasn't connected to a higher purpose may have been the actual problem.

I found what was missing a few years ago when I attended a retreat for women. My friend had suggested that I go because I was at a point where I wanted to make some big life changes but I didn't really know where to start. Confident about my relationships and my home life, I was feeling very uncertain about my chosen career and was beginning to lack focus and commitment. I really struggled with thoughts of leaving because I had a significant sense of loyalty to the company where I had worked since graduating from university. I was spinning my wheels and decided to take that weekend to reconnect with myself in a way that I hadn't in a very long time. What I gained from the retreat was miraculous. My life has not been the same since.

Various exercises, group and individual, led the particpants on a journey of self-inquiry. We were asked some serious questions that had many of us questioning the "truths" we had held so long about what we were meant to be in this world. For me, personally, there was one activity that provided insight like no other. After reviewing a lengthy list, I had to identify my top ten values. This was the toughest thing I had to do all weekend. I hadn't before given any thought to what was really important to me. I suppose, on a subconscious level, I knew that family, friends, and happiness were important values of mine, but I had never considered how my life could be structured to honour them. In this exercise, I had to analyze my life and provide evidence for those values. This was a real eye-opener! While it was clear that the priority I had subconsciously set for family and friends was in alignment with my daily life, there was nothing that connected my work with my values.

At first I was shocked, but as the retreat leader lead me through the process, it all made sense. The growing dissatisfaction that I was experiencing at work was a direct result of the fact that it did not align with my values. The stress, the anxiety, and the discomfort were all manifestations of my failure to connect on a deep level with the work I was doing every day. "Does this mean I have to leave my job?" I asked. "Not necessarily," came the reply, "but this is your opportunity to make changes to reconnect your life to your personal values."

Again, it was amazing to learn that I didn't even *have* to change my job in order to increase my satisfaction there and my happiness overall. The rest of the morning I spent time figuring out how to honour my values in my current job. I was incredibly empowered at the thought of reinventing my experience in the office, even though I would be essentially doing the same things every day. I learned that the difference was not in what I would be *doing*, but how I was *being*. Being connected, being conscious, and being aware would change my perception. I would move out of victimhood and into a life where I was purposeful. That is something that had been missing for a while and I was determined to do whatever I could to get it back.

Years have passed since my friend and I went to that retreat. I have become a student of our leader and truly embraced her philosophies. The results I have had are incredible. By reconnecting with my purpose and aligning my outer world with my core values, I am content and fulfilled. I am inspired each day to contribute my best to my family and friends. I love my work. I am still at the same company but I've gotten a promotion to a position that is a better expression of my skills, abilities, and values. I never would have had the courage to pursue something different within the same company if I hadn't gotten clear about what was important to me. I am so grateful for the lessons I have learned. I promise to never forget.

What if they knew I am connected?

I am Nurturing

As a mother, I am experiencing one of life's greatest gifts: I am nurturing another human being to his potential. From the time my son was conceived, this was a role that I willingly accepted with all my heart. It is unlike any role you will play. The influence is instant and everlasting. It is daunting. It is the biggest challenge of my life. It is the most rewarding.

Even before my son was born, I began the nurturing process. I took better care of my health as I prepared for motherhood. I ate healthy; I took vitamins; I exercised; I read. I was deliberate in everything I chose to think, do and feel. Of course, once I became pregnant, I continued down this road but with a greater sense of purpose and vigilance. Purpose is what motherhood gives you. You are automatically responsible for another being, and in the first nine months, it literally breathes the same air as you. Talk about pressure! But it doesn't feel like that. To an Impressive Woman, this is the project we've been preparing for our whole lives. *Why do you think we played with dolls?* In preparation for the big game, that's why. And, now it's here and there is no turning back.

My job as a mother is to nurture my son—to be a witness to his growth and development—until such time as he leaves the home. [There is a debate in our house about when that will actually happen. My mother tells me that the apron strings are never cut but I tell my son that he's out once college is finished and sooner if he studies abroad.] There are things I must teach him. There are things he can only learn from me (or at least that's where I would prefer that he learn them). I've given some thought to

149

what I want to teach my son before he strikes out on his own [at age 18, 22, or God forbid, 35]. This list is not all inclusive, of course, but highlights many the things that I consider to be my responsibility:

- It's ok to express your feelings
- Be respectful
- Mind your manners
- Always do what you say you are going to do when you say you are going to do it
- Pick up after yourself
- You are responsible for the success you achieve
- Follow your heart
- Treat women with admiration and adoration (hold doors, buy presents, make plans)
- Pursue your dreams
- Surround yourself with successful people
- Know what you value and build a life around that
- Share your wealth
- Love with all your heart (even if it might get broken)
- Take risks (but do the math first)
- Ask for help when you need it
- Be there for your family and friends
- Don't take advantage; don't take for granted
- Be kind

As his mother, I believe that it is my responsibility to teach my son these lessons. It will be my privilege. He'll learn his own along the way, too. I know that there will be disappointments, failures, sadness and grief in his life, even though I don't like to admit it. I wish I could shelter him from the bad things but that wouldn't be serving him at all. He has to face his journey in his own time and at his own speed. All I can do is lay a foundation so that, if he gets lost, he knows there is a place to return to that is safe and full of love.

What if they knew I am nurturing?

I Surrender

What would your world look like if you let go of the need to be right? What if, for one day, you surrendered all judgment? What do you suppose would happen to your relationships, your workplace, and your home life? How would you feel inside?

Letting go of preconceived ideas is more difficult for some than others. This continues to be the area of my ego that challenges me most. As a reformed perfectionist, it is easy for me to slip back into old patterns of judgment, where I find fault OR excellence in all things. My mind is a judging machine! Even my Myers Briggs profile, ENFJ, tells me I am, so I must be, right?? There I go again!

Yes, I have been right many times and when I am not as sure, I gather evidence (like the MB typing above) to back me up. I have surrounded myself with people that support my views and avoided those who challenge me. My type A personality (more evidence) has had me so wound up when the world around me appears "wrong" that I can barely cope. I have manifested illnesses like chronic back pain and headaches as I fight the concept of surrender: Wouldn't that make me wrong?? Wait, isn't THAT another judgment?

I feel like I have been typing in circles. I apologize for that to the reader who is trying to pick some sense out of this confession. The fact is that, without surrendering judgment, our minds do create vicious cycles that are difficult to stop. Once we decide that we are right, it automatically makes someone else wrong. What good can come from that? When we are in the cycle of judgment, we can easily miss the beauty of the imperfection of life.

If we remove the ultimate word of judgment, "should", from our vocabulary, freedom will reign. Think about it! How many times each day do you find yourself saying things like:

- I really should do the dishes now.
- The kids should do their homework now.
- My spouse should fix this now.
- My dad should mind his own business.
- My neighbour should take better care of …

Alright, already. I surrender! For one day, I will surrender just to see what happens. I do believe that the peace that I will find will catapult this Impressive Woman to a place she has never been. It is a place I am willing to go. I am willing to risk it and take the journey into the unknown. *Will you come with me?*

When we surrender judgment, we have a remarkable opportunity to learn about ourselves. How we judge others is often how we perceive ourselves to be lacking. If we judge another to be stupid, fat, or ugly, it often comes from a deeper self-image issue that we need to address in ourselves. When we judge others to be imperfect, we are projecting the feeling of imperfection that we view in ourselves, even if we do so unconsciously. It is imperative (is that a judgment?) that we look inward to the source of our insecurities that ultimately causes us to form judgments. Think of the awesome power there is to reclaim when we accept what is and surrender the need to be right.

Imagine if we recognized the divine beauty in all people and all things, accepting that how we see them is actually different than how others do. This is part of what makes this a wonderful world! We are blessed with the capacity to change our minds and change our worlds.

From this day forward, I will embrace the imperfect because it is there where beauty lies. I will respond with compassion and love. I will do this for myself first, then for others. I will move forward with an open heart to what is possible and there, I will be rewarded with the inner peace that has eluded me for my entire life.

What if they knew I surrender?

I am Tolerant

I believe that, as an Impressive Woman, one of the most important qualities you can possess is to be tolerant. There are some people who are born tolerant, to be sure. I can accept the notion that everyone is actually born tolerant but that we learn from our families and societies that intolerance is acceptable and soon, we have become tainted and prejudiced. With this in mind, I believe that is what happened to me and that, as a young adult, I chose, quite deliberately, to relearn the virtue of tolerance and that decision has served me well.

Growing up in a small village, I was not exposed to different races or religions. I didn't even know there were people of different colors or convictions until I had to travel 30 minutes up the highway to go to middle school in the nearest town. This town was no booming metropolis but people there looked strange to me. I had heard that they had different churches there, that the fathers weren't all fisherman, and that some of the mothers had jobs. This was all very shocking to me. I didn't know what to think but I was soon taught. I was told, "Don't listen to them. They're different." *Different* meant bad or ignorant. *Different* meant dangerous.

I went through my teenage years feeling very frightened and confused. In my heart, it pained me that I couldn't be friends with the girls who were in my class. They seemed nice. I didn't understand why my parents didn't want me to go to dances. I was not allowed to spend any time in the town except when I was at school. I was not expected to leave the village once I graduated high school.

Eventually, I learned, on my own, that there was a big, beautiful world out there full of people and possibilities that were different than what I was experiencing at home. At first, I felt ashamed of my curiosity and this deep yearning to learn what made people look, speak, and act differently. That sense of shame could not keep me down once I reached the end of my school days and I claimed my freedom to explore the world.

I left home with a sense of exhilaration that I had never known. I vowed that I would embrace the differences of everyone I met. It dawned on me that if I was harbouring judgment against other people without even knowing them, people could be discriminating against me. I could not stand for such ignorance. I had been surrounded by it my whole life.

To this day, I am proud of the place I call home and the hard-working people of that fishing village. I love them for who they are. I understand now that intolerance comes from ignorance and when you live in isolation, it is easy to fear the unknown and build walls in an effort to protect your own way of life. I forgive those who taught me that it was best to live this way because they did not know any other way. I choose, however, to live differently. And *different* is good. *Different* is meant to be celebrated!

What if they knew I am tolerant?

I am Awesome

ANDREA, 25

I read "The Book of Awesome" over the holidays and it got me to thinking: I could write a list of all the reasons that I am awesome! I did vet this by one of my best friends before posting just to ensure I wasn't making stuff up. This page isn't really long enough to cover it all so I decided to focus on the things that I think make me special; that is, those qualities that I think make me an Impressive Woman and not just your Average Jane. *How awesome am I?*

I am reliable. You can count on me. It doesn't matter if it's raining, I will meet you for dinner if I said I would. I will also help you move. I will help you with your school project. Whatever I said I will do, I will do. I have integrity.

I know how to have fun. When we are together, you can be sure that we will have a good time. I love to laugh. I love to make other people smile and enjoy themselves. I am prepared to be silly when the situation calls for it. I am willing to dress up in costumes and ask strangers to dance. I will play board games and add flavour to popcorn. I will run through the sprinkler and throw water balloons. What a riot!

I will make your day. It's your birthday? I'll hire a singing telegram. Your turtle died? Here's the perfect sympathy card. Your boyfriend's being a jerk? I have chocolate. You're swamped at work? I brought your favourite casserole into the office and a little nip of wine to wash it down. Your house is a mess? I love to organize! You have a hot date? I am the most fun babysitter in the world... and I'm free!

I'm listening. Come and sit on my couch. We will drink tea (or wine) and you can pour out your heart and soul. I am here for you. I will not judge you. I will not give advice. I will not tell stories about when the same thing happened to me. I will hold you while you cry. I will tell you everything is going to be ok.

I am here to help. I've got a different perspective than you and that means that I have different ideas that can fix your problem. I want nothing more than to ease your pain. Without expectation, I will provide suggestions and feedback so that you can choose how to proceed from here. I have your best interest at heart. Trust me.

I love you. If you are in my life, I love you. Because I love you, it is my intention to make your life better. I will anticipate your needs as best I can, and I will surprise you with tokens of affection, big and small. I adore you and want you to be in my life forever. I want you to always feel secure in that knowledge so I communicate openly and honestly.

What if they knew that I am awesome?

I am Positive

I am a positive person. I always have been. Every day when I wake up, I look outside and thank God that I am alive to see another day. I never take for granted this privilege because I know, first hand, how quickly life can end and that, when your time is done, you don't have any say in the matter.

Sadly, I know what it is to lose someone at young age, before her time was up. It can be easy, some would say even *natural*, to lose yourself in grief and to question the meaning of it all. I had those moments, to be sure, but I chose to remain positive because *I* am still here and I have been given the opportunity to make a difference. What good would it do me or those around me if I shut down? What purpose would it serve if I chose to quit living? We are all put on this earth for an indeterminate amount of time and I believe that is a privilege. It is a gift that I intend to honour by being a positive influence every single day.

Looking out the window on a cold winter's day, I choose to stay positive. Today is the perfect day to stay inside and cuddle, go outside and make a snowman with the kids, or re-organize my closet. I am grateful. My attitude has the power to change lives and I take that responsibility very seriously. At the breakfast table, how I choose to be will influence the tone of the conversation, what is said, and how my family will feel. The impact lasts much longer than the cereal and juice. The positive energy provides a foundation for our day.

By starting the day off on a positive note, I carry myself in love and light and I spread it wherever I go. I greet people warmly and use my manners. I acknowledge the contribution of the people in my life. I recognize the contribution of my family, friends, and coworkers who make my life full and satisfying. I love being a positive influence in their lives and I have been blessed to attract people who do the same for me.

I have been challenged, like I said, because bad things still happen to good people. I feel sad and angry when they do. Positive people are not living in glass bubbles. We are simply conscious of the effect that our energy has on the world and we have made a decision to make it count for good. As long as I am on this earth, I will make it my mission to spread positivity wherever I go. This is my calling. As an Impressive Woman, and as a human being who has been "left behind" by others whose time may have come too early, I feel it is my duty.

What if they knew I am positive?

I am a Dreamer

On the eve of my 38th birthday, I finally know what I want. You know how, at each birthday, you are told to make a wish when you blow out your candles? Well, for 37 birthdays in a row, I have drawn a blank. Perhaps I always held, deep inside me, a core belief that dreams don't come true. Perhaps that is why I never allowed myself to think about a future filled with gumdrops and bubble gum, or convertibles and Gucci handbags. I know better now. I know that dreams do come true and that wisdom has set me free to dream big!

I learned a valuable lesson recently that changed my belief that dreams only come true for other people. I learned that life hadn't been happening *to* me but I had actually been creating my reality all along! I had never thought about that before. When I learned that *your outer world reflects your inner world*, it was the biggest "light-bulb moment" I had ever had. Before, I couldn't see the connection between my negative thoughts and the disappointing results in my life. While I appeared as the Impressive Woman when I was at work and with my friends, I always felt like I was fighting an uphill battle. I felt that I had to prove myself, to work harder than anyone else, that I would only be rewarded if I was ten times better than the next person. I was exhausted because I was constantly struggling. I did not know that my mindset alone–these beliefs that had been ingrained for a lifetime–were sabotaging my efforts to create a fulfilling life.

The good news is that I am now clear about the power that I have to create a life that inspires me every day. I have given myself permission to stop the struggle and to embrace my journey, whatever it brings. I believe that it will bring love, happiness, and contribution because that is my dream. Even writing these words fill me up with a sense of pride for finally seeing the truth! The truth is that I don't have to be the CEO to make a valuable contribution to my company. The truth is that I don't have to be a mother to nurture and care for others. The truth is that I don't have to be a millionaire in order to take a European vacation each year. I know that all of these things are possible; all of these dreams can come true. There is so much more that I want in my life and I now know that changing my mindset is the first step to making those dreams a reality.

On my birthday, I will make a wish as I blow out my 38 candles. In fact, I may make several. In preparation, I am going to start a list of all the things I have ever wanted but was afraid to say out loud. I am going to make a Dream Board and post pictures of my dream vacation spots, home, car, and lover. I am inspired. I will dream because I am worthy. I will manifest my dreams because I believe in my power.

What if they knew I am a dreamer?

I am Inspired

I listened to a woman speak at a conference last weekend and I have been forever changed. Her story inspired me to step into my true power as an Impressive Woman and create the life of my dreams. She taught me that there are no limits besides those that you create in your mind. Why didn't I see this before?

I could stay stuck here in this moment, beating myself up for not having seen this before. I could commiserate over the lost years on the Treadmill of Life, forever running and not getting any closer to my dreams, but why would I spend more negative energy in that place? No, I choose to ride this wave of inspiration because now *it is my time*. I don't think I was really ready to embrace this message until now. I am so excited about the possibilities that lie ahead that I feel like I am floating.

To get myself grounded, I am going to meditate. The speaker suggested that we spend quiet time alone each day to connect with our Higher Self. I hadn't ever made this a part of my daily routine but I am starting now because it feels like the best way to honour myself. Connecting in silence, she says, will create a space for new ideas and solutions to enter into my consciousness. I can see that, in the past, my mind has always been too full to allow for inspiration. I'm game. I sit in the silence, listen to my breath, and ask for guidance. *Where do I go from here? What is my heart's desire? Who do I want to be in this world?*

I am beginning a new leg of this journey of life and I feel empowered. Thanks to this wonderful speaker, I have gained a fresh perspective. I used to spend a lot of time in judgment of other people and myself, too. I had even looked upon this speaker in judgment, putting her up on a pedestal, thinking she was better than me. I didn't even know her! For as long as I can remember, I carried a belief that some were more worthy of success than others. I came to the realization that this *lie* had prevented me from forming solid relationships and creating wealth.

I am no more or less worthy than anyone. We all want the same things: love, security, a sense of belonging and contribution. And we are all deserving.

Through my meditation I see that there is a little girl with a dream inside of this Impressive Woman. I honour her by making the connection. She is full of light and love. She is full of promise. She wants you to create a wonderful life because you deserve it. I tell seven-year-old Ida the words I have longed to hear: "You are perfect just the way you are. I love you."

What if they knew I am inspired?

I am Creative

My goodness, I am simply in awe of myself. Truly, when I become the observer of myself, I am able to recognize how creative I am. It is remarkable. It took a while for me to see this in myself, although it was always something I noticed right away in others.

I have always surrounded myself with people who demonstrated a kind of artistic talent. Whether they were potters, painters, dancers, or musicians, they shared a passion for performance of one kind or another that was an authentic expression of their identity. At least, that is how I saw it. You may look at it differently. You may see a drummer in a rock band as some dude who's banging away maniacally and trying to make a few extra bucks while looking for a "real" job. I see someone with a gift who is channelling from the divine. It is creativity without bounds. I can lose myself watching artists the way they lose themselves in the process.

Lost in the process is the wrong way to capture it because I ultimately *find* myself in the creative process. As I open myself up to guidance from my Higher Self, I become deeply connected with the essence of Catherine. I am focused. I am on fire. I am untouchable. I can create from nothing and this is awe-inspiring. Again, because I recognize and celebrate this gift in artists of all genres, I do not feel this is an egotistical remark. I believe that we must first love our own work if we are to feel comfortable sharing it with others. Sharing it with others is what the most successful artists do.

There is an incredible amount of satisfaction found when sharing your gift with people who appreciate the creative process.

Visit any theatre and ask the best actors why they do what they do. There is an admirable quality that shines through as they acknowledge their gift and love to bring it to life so that others may be inspired by their performance. It is the same for artisans, painters, and singers. What they create—the beautiful, the remarkable—comes from a spark of inspiration that often cannot be traced to anything tangible. In a momentary flicker of insight, a small idea turns into greatness. What's not to admire about that? And then there's the hard work that goes into the process.

When I look back over my lifetime as an artist, I see the patterns in my life—those times when I was at my peak and those times when I struggled. Because my livelihood is derived from my creative expression, it is fundamental to my existence that I create every day. In order to facilitate this, I have deliberately and masterfully created the perfect environment. For example, knowing that I get most of my inspiration from nature, I have chosen to live in a house in the woods, surrounded by hiking trails and backing onto a lake. Just peering out the window or strolling around the property will ground me and connect me in such a way that I open the channel to let inspiration come in. My days are structured so that communing with nature is a priority. I work best in solitude, so my studio is set apart from the rest of the house, away from the office and the high traffic areas. I have decorated my creative space with colors and images that boost my energy and confidence. Here, I am at home. At home is how I feel when I am tapping into the well of creativity that is me.

I have started to talk with other artists about their processes and how they make the connection to enhance creativity. I feel that, as an Impressive Woman, I have a duty to share my success and encourage others to step into their power. It is such a blessing to be able to make a living in such a unique way. Artists bring beauty and light into the world. Actually, we all do. We are all creative. Is it lovely?

What if they knew I am creative?

I am Receptive

What does it mean to be receptive? I didn't know until a few years ago when I came face to face with the realization that success doesn't have to be a struggle if I would only *allow* it to come my way. My whole life had been spent *making things happen* and it never occurred to me that it would be easier to just invite happiness in.

I had this chip on my shoulder that I carried with me since I was a kid. I was one of five children in my family, and the only girl. I felt I had to constantly prove to everyone that I was competent, capable, and in control. I didn't want them to think any less of me because I was of the "fairer" sex. I didn't want them to think I was weak so I took on more challenges than anyone in their right mind and I worked myself into frenzy until I prevailed. And I always did. *That would show them!*

But even after I left home, started a family and began a promising career, I didn't give up that struggle. I kept working like I had something to prove until I was well into my forties. By then, I was exhausted. I hit a wall. I actually got really sick. I was in need of help and not just to heal my physical body but to heal this limiting belief that had burdened me for so long.

I needed to be released from the chains that were holding me hostage. This way of being was damaging my health and my relationships, too. I had come to a point of no return; that's when I discovered the truth. A practitioner in holistic medicine helped me come to terms with what my choices had created. I took responsibility and committed to a new way of being. I had to do it. The risk of not changing was too great. This doctor helped me see that there was a greater power that was co-creating my world with me. If I had enough faith in that power and in myself, the success would come to me naturally, without me having to force it with all my might.

As so it is. For many years now I have been living the life of an Impressive Woman and it is all because I have allowed goodness to enter my life naturally and without force. I came to terms with the destructive nature of my patterns and let them go—not by working hard, but simply receiving. I also forgave myself and my family. That was part of the healing process. After my mind and spirit was cleansed, I felt renewed and re-awakened. I felt like myself, only better than I ever have. I opened myself up to all that was possible and I was rewarded.

I am now a master at manifesting what I desire. My life has changed dramatically but not so much on the outside as on the inside. I had always had the trappings of success—the home, the family, the car, the vacations—but I never had the sense of gratitude and contentment that comes when you live your life with higher consciousness. The day that I gave up the struggle and embraced a higher power was the day that I first felt like I had arrived. What an amazing gift!

What if they knew I am receptive?

I am Fun

Anyone up for a dip? That's me. Always the life of the party. I love to have fun and love being the one who makes it all happen. I have a reputation as an Impressive Woman and one of my most distinguishing characteristics is that I am so much fun!

I like to find opportunity in every situation to make it more enjoyable. I don't believe there is any such thing as having too much fun. Now, I'm talking about good, clean fun, here. I don't partake in anything sleazy, underhanded, or shenanigans that make people uncomfortable. I don't make jokes at other people's expense.

Sometimes people get the wrong impression and think I'm up for that kind of stuff. I'm not. I always take the high road and I make my boundaries known. Just because I will go skinny-dipping with my girlfriends, doesn't mean that I'll do it with their husbands! If I did, I think I'd be seriously risking my reputation as an Impressive Woman and as the most fun girl on the block. Not interested.

One of my core values is fun so I make a conscious effort to bring it with me everywhere. Here are just a few things I have done to incorporate fun into my world:

- *In my car.* I have the cutest bobble head of a Hawaiian hula dancer. It reminds me, too, that I need to get my butt to Hawaii and learn how to do that!
- *On my desk.* I have a daily calendar featuring funny cartoons that make me laugh out loud at the beginning of every day.

- *On my computer.* My screensaver is a picture of me and my friends wearing sombreros and drinking tequila on our girls' trip to Mexico.
- *In my stereo.* A playlist that reminds me of high school dances. I always sing and dance along.
- *In my bedroom.* The song that wakes me up every morning as my alarm clock goes off also makes me laugh before my eyes are even open.
- *On my wall.* Photos that capture my family at a recent reunion where we played horse shoes, ran a three-legged race, and kicked butt in the big scavenger hunt.
- *On my patio.* Strings of lights are up all year round indicating to my neighbours that my house is where the fun is happening all the time, so come on over!
- *In my closet.* There is a separate compartment that holds costumes for occasions such as Mardi Gras, Christmas, St. Patrick's Day, or Easter. I can also be ready at the drop of a hat to participate in belly dancing, karate, windsurfing, rock climbing, ballroom dancing, or a murder mystery dinner party. How cool is that?

What if they knew I am fun?

I am Adventuresome

I believe that one of the main reasons people consider me to be an Impressive Woman is that I am so adventuresome. I am willing to try anything once; twice, if I liked it! I really enjoy seeking out new and exciting things to do in my spare time and I love bringing like-minded souls along for the ride.

I have travelled to four continents and seen the most magnificent sites. I have eaten delicious food that I didn't recognize and couldn't pronounce. I have rented mopeds and hired mountain guides who barely spoke English. I have walked in the steps of ancient philosophers and I have stood in front of the most incredibly innovative architecture on the planet. I have learned to say hello in more than 20 languages but asking for directions has been more challenging. I find that, with patience, an open heart, and a bright smile, you will eventually get where you are going—or you will discover something off the beaten path that was definitely worth the detour.

Right here, in my own backyard, I have hiked and biked to some of the most remote, and most breath-taking places in the world. I am so blessed to have access to a bounty of natural wonders whenever the mood strikes me—which is often, I admit. Because travel is expensive, and due to the fact that I have a regular job, I cannot travel abroad more than a couple of times a year so I strategize to bring my sense of adventure into my everyday life as much as possible. In addition to strategically choosing where I live, I have fashioned my life around this part of my personality; I have found it to be the key to my happiness.

From a practical point of view, I want to be ready when the next opportunity for adventure arises. I have one whole closet devoted to "travel clothes": comfortable, easy to pack, versatile, and neutral in color. I've got outerwear and underwear; shoes, boots, and sandals; hats, caps, and helmets; knapsacks, backpacks, and canteens. My garage contains all the gear I need for camping, kayaking and cycling. I've joined several clubs in town that are devoted to different hobbies connected to the outdoors and travel, too, so I can stay in the conversation and continually learn about new things to try.

In my house, I have a separate room where I meditate and do yoga. It is also where I do all my travel planning. In this space, which is decorated with objects from all over the world and photos chronicling my adventures, I am able to transport myself as I visualize where I want to go and what I want to experience. While being adventuresome carries with it a degree of spontaneity, I do spend a significant amount of time in preparation for the next big trip. I have a cabinet that holds all my travel documents. With these things, I am meticulously organized.

Honouring this aspect of my personality has created great meaning in my life. I am happy to share my enthusiasm for adventure with other people to inspire them to trying new things and expand their perspectives. It is a very liberal way to live. It is also very joyful. You should try it!

What if they knew I am adventuresome?

I Believe

I believe in miracles. I believe that when you pray, you are heard. I probably wouldn't have believed, except that I have witnessed many miracles over the years. "I used to be a skeptic, but I'm alright now," I have been known to retort when anyone else thinks that I am full of crap. I pray for them, too. I pray that they will see the truth.

In faith, there is freedom; you are released from carrying the burden of working out all your problems on your own. When I surrender–let go and Let God, as it were–I feel lighter. I am an Impressive Woman; I hold a great deal of responsibility at home and at work. I used to worry all the time about how things would ever get resolved. I would spend sleepless nights eating through buckets of ice cream and fretful days swallowing Aspirin and Tums to feign off the headaches and heartburn. On the fateful day when I became a believer, I threw out all the painkillers in my house and office, and never relied on them again.

I had hit a wall. I was struggling to make a few things right in my life: personality conflicts at work; communication issues with my boyfriend; the accumulation of too much debt; weight gain. And, then I had a personal health crisis. My doctor told me that if I didn't get my stress levels under control, I'd have to be medicated for the rest of my life. It scared the crap out of me! I figured that something had to change because if I kept doing the same things that I had been doing, I would keep getting the same results. Expecting something different is what Einstein called insanity. I wasn't ready for the Funny Farm yet!

So I mustered up all the faith and confidence I could find, and I did something I had never done before... I let go! I wrote in my journal a declaration. I was turning over all of my worries to a higher power, the One that had a greater plan. I asked for a miracle. I asked for help. I decided that I would live the best way I knew how but that I would allow space for miracles to enter and solve my problems. I admitted that I didn't know the answers and that I needed divine intervention so that I could be all I was meant to be. I was desperate and I believed with all my heart that I was on the path to freedom.

I was right. The help did come. The answers to my problems came in ways that I never would have manifested if I had forced the issue. People who had just the right skills showed up to fix problems at work. Out of the blue, other people dropped out of my life and toxic relationships ended. I met a wonderful coach who helped me change my patterns of eating and, with her support, I quickly adopted a new healthy lifestyle that left me feeling empowered; I also began to lose my excess weight. My stress levels dropped as I gave thanks every day to the miracles that were surrounding me.

Now that my life is seemingly "under control", I continue to give thanks each day for the miracle that is life. When I do face challenges, I remember to ask for help and believe in miracles. There is no reason for struggle. Embrace the notion that there is a Higher Power that will send you the answers you seek when you open yourself up to the possibility.

What if they knew I believe?

I am Privileged

There is no question that the greatest gifts that have been bestowed on me are also the biggest miracles: my two children. My life has been forever altered because I am their mother. There isn't a day that goes by that I don't thank God for their presence. I am mindful of the privilege it is to raise them, nurture them, and love them with all of my heart.

Several years ago, when their father and I divorced, the children began to live with me on a part-time basis. This decision was the fairest for both parents but it didn't make it any easier. I would no longer be able to tuck them in, make their breakfast in the morning, and share afterschool milk and cookies with them on a daily basis. My life took on a new reality—one where I am a single woman with no attachments one week and a full-time parent the next.

In ways I have "the best of both worlds". I have one week where I can focus entirely on the children because I no longer have to share them. I have become much more conscious of how we spend our time. We do whatever pleases us. I choose not to do major household chores like laundry, cleaning, and vacuuming when I have the children. I choose instead to concentrate on making memories. Each weeknight, we enjoy dinner and our favourite TV shows or go outdoors to shoot hoops or ride our bikes. On the weekends, we take full-day outings to the museums, park or beach. I also try to fit in one-on-one time with each child throughout the week. I feel this is very important in order to establish an open and communicative relationship with each of them. They are very different children with different needs and wants. It is my job to honour them and I take that responsibility very seriously.

On my solo weeks, I busy myself with all the household chores that were left undone when I had the children and I keep myself occupied with my own interests. Having this space to reconnect with myself in the silence has been very good for my personal development and mental health. The space also allows me to miss them greatly and be aware of the importance of deliberately making "our time" quality time.

As much as I miss my children when they are away from me, I have grown used to this arrangement (as have they) and I am grateful. During that time, I am able to care for myself, rest and rejuvenate, and make plans for our time together. I am more present with them than most parents are and I know that they benefit from a parent who is fully engaged. As difficult as it was to file for divorce, I know that I could not have been as a good a mother to the children if I had stayed married to their father. I was not happy in that relationship and, therefore, I was never at my best. Sure, I did what I could and tried my hardest, but one cannot compare the influence of a woman who feels like a victim to an Impressive Woman who loves herself and her life.

It may seem odd, but this arrangement has been the catalyst for me to become a better parent. I am blessed to have co-created two of the most amazing creatures in this world. I cherish them and have grown to like them very much. My kids roll their eyes at me and say, "Mom, what do you mean, you like us? We know you *love* us." And I smile, "I *have* to love you because I'm your mother. I *like* you because of the great people you are." No matter how often we share that exchange, it's never too much. It always ends with, "Mom, we like you, too."

What if they knew I am privileged?

I am Successful

How do *you* define success? It only matters to you, doesn't it? I came to that brilliant realization when I was an Impressive Woman of 30 and then, I spent the next 20 years getting clear about what success means to me and making it a reality. While I've had my share of ups and downs, I see it all as part of the journey I was meant to take. I am grateful for every experience because it brought me to here and this is a pretty fantastic place to be. At 50 years old, I can say that I am truly embracing my potential. Here are the keys to my success:

Clarity. I have become crystal clear on what success means to me. It has changed over the years because my priorities have changed. My core values haven't, however, and once I figured out what they were, I always ensured that they were front and center in any grand vision that I held for myself. I have used techniques like journaling, vision boards, and meditation to help me focus on what I really want. It is amazing how well it all works when you are deliberate about getting clear.

Commitment. Once I determined what success looked like for me, I set about to make it happen. In order to get results, however, I knew that my commitment had to be solid. I posted notes all over the house—on the bathroom mirror, on the fridge, in my appointment book, on the answering machine—that said things like, "You did it! Way to go! You rock! You made it!" to remind myself that I was going down this road for a reason: *I was worth it.* When I was faced with challenges and tempted to waver, I remembered those funny little sticky notes all over the house and the promise that I made to myself. Why would I go back on my word? I am the most important person in my life, for goodness sake.

Choice. With a clear vision and a strong commitment, all I had to do was make choices that aligned with my definition of success and I had it made. When I started to track the number of decisions I consciously made every day, I had to stop! Seriously, it was taking up too much time. I did it for a week or so just so that I would have "proof" that I was taking this commitment to heart. It was also useful on days when my faith would drop and I was starting to forget the point of it all. One morning, before work, I had already recorded a list that looked like this: smiled when I got out of bed, kissed my husband right away, admired myself in the mirror, went for a run, ate a healthy breakfast, and enjoyed a hot bath. Do you see what I mean? Making mental notes was much more efficient!

Confidence. What I love about having to make so many choices is that you have the opportunity to create success each time. Yes, every choice that you make that is in alignment with your vision is a success in itself. As you celebrate each little success, your confidence grows. And that increases the likelihood that you will continue to make healthy choices. By the same token, your confidence is negatively affected when you make choices that do not support your long-term vision. Sometimes we are not consciously aware of how we are affected by the decisions because we are not even conscious of most things that we choose, but our bodies tell us through pain, dis-ease and discomfort. Check in with your body. Does it say you are successful?

Community. The final piece of the success puzzle is to build a community of support. I was smart enough to communicate with my family and friends very early on in the process, to let them know of my vision of success. I came right out and told them, "I want your support and if you want to be in my life, you must be there when I need someone to lean on or to celebrate." I gave them the choice. I was fortunate to have their support from the beginning but I admit that they didn't always "get" what I was trying to accomplish so I went on to establish a greater community that held similar interests and ambitions. In this age of social media, it is really easy to connect with like-minded people. I suggest that you do this. But I also think there's nothing better than a mastermind group with accountability partners who support your vision and keep your feet to the fire. That's just how I roll.

I challenge anyone to take these five steps seriously and not create a life of their dreams. Together, these elements capture everything you need to design a life of success. Remember it is *your* definition that counts, just like mine serves me. I wouldn't have it any other way.

What if they knew I am successful?

I am Compassionate

Do you cry when you watch those World Vision commercials on TV? I do. I can't get through them without tearing up and, sometimes, I actually sob. It's hard to imagine that this kind of hardship exists in a world that, from my perspective, appears so abundant. As an Impressive Woman, I am surrounded with indicators of wealth. That is what I have attracted. It doesn't make me vain, however. It doesn't make me better than anyone else. It makes me more compassionate.

Before I had any of this wealth, I worked very hard to keep my financial head above water. I came from an average home where my parents borrowed for big purchases and chose to "do without" when our budget couldn't handle our wants. I adopted this perspective of money for a long time and struggled away. When I was in a place of lack myself, and always thinking about what I couldn't afford, I didn't have the emotional capacity to be compassionate to another person's misfortune.

Fortunately, I wasn't too far into my twenties when I stepped into a more positive mindset and learned that to attract wealth, you must think wealthy thoughts. Seemingly overnight, everything changed. Because I had experienced such dramatic changes in my finances, I was driven to help others find the same abundance. First, I had to open my eyes widely to see how widespread the problems were. Then, I made a deliberate choice to help certain organizations whose missions were in alignment with my own values. I felt confident that I had something of value to contribute, so I contacted them and offered to help in my own unique way.

The organizations that I approached were all grateful for the assistance. I have chosen to contribute my skills, talents, abilities, and finances in different ways, depending on what they need and always in consultation. Just because I am an Impressive Woman, I do not have the understanding of their needs; I do not have all the answers. I have donated money when that was the best thing to do. I have organized fundraisers because I am really good at that and I have a significant social network in the city. I have also delivered free seminars on empowerment to the members of their communities.

In all cases, the people I served were touched by my compassion. They knew my story and were truly grateful that I had chosen to act. My own life transformation moved me to put my money where my mouth is and make a difference in the lives of others. It takes compassion to a whole other level when you can see the results of your own contribution. The satisfaction of helping others succeed is out of this world. It is priceless.

What if they knew I am compassionate?

I Have Purpose

My husband's employer required that we relocate across the country with our two children, all with six week's notice. This was the first time we would have to make such a move but we weren't sure if it would be the last. His company was experiencing significant growth and he played an integral part in the success of his product line. If they continue to expand in other areas of the country, we may be packing our bags again. But that could be years from now, and I had more immediate concerns. I had a purpose. And I was grateful for that.

For the past few years, I had been feeling disconnected from myself. I had been working a part-time job just to make a bit of spending money and get me out of the house a few days a week. It helped to pay for our family vacations but it was really unfulfilling and I was feeling quite uninspired of late. This arrangement was fine when the kids were younger but now that they are hitting the teenage years, I have really been looking for something more. A project is what I need, I thought. Well, that's exactly what I got with this relocation. I quit my job and dedicated the next several months to making this transition as easy and as rewarding as possible for my family.

I've always been very organized so the logistical aspects of the move were not concerning me at all. I knew all of that would fall into place. What was truly exciting to me was the opportunity to create a brand new life for our family. We were always happy *enough*, but I saw this move as an adventure, a way to really ramp up the happiness quotient in our lives. I planned to take this project on with deliberate intent and truly enjoy the process.

The first thing I did was to call a family meeting. Because I live with three males, I gave them advance warning of the meeting and told them they would be expected to participate. I warned them, as well, that we would be talking about feelings. Despite, their initial trepidation, they all agreed to give it a shot. [They are so wonderful!] I asked my husband and the boys to share their concerns about the move, their fears, and their perceptions. Then I asked them to describe their ideal home and way of life, without regard to where we were living. It was really interesting. I took my turn and told them that I had found my purpose. From that moment on, I would be devoted to creating a new life for our family that finds each one of us connected and fulfilled. I would create an atmosphere in our home that was conducive to meeting the needs of everyone.

Everyone went away from the meeting feeling a bit buzzed. It was thrilling for me to connect with each of the boys on such a deep level. I wanted to do my best to honour their dreams for a great new life on the other side of the country. I started out by making a vision board that would capture all of our sentiments and aspirations. It really looked fantastic. I had pictures of activities we wanted to do, paint chips, electronics for the games room, the garden, the big barbecue, friends who would visit, laughter, and love. Just looking at the vision board transported me to our new life and gave me feelings of satisfaction, contribution, and happiness. I noticed that the guys also looked at it each day. They would add pictures, too. One of my sons actually made his own. I knew that it was really helping them feel grounded and not overwhelmed with all that was still unknown.

The funny thing is that our vision board was the last thing to be packed into the moving truck. It had its own box so it would be the first thing removed. I wanted it to remind us, throughout the adventure of our relocation, of all that is possible. Now that we are settled, the boys are in school and my husband has been brought up to speed in the new office, life has resumed a familiar pace. I still remember my purpose, however, and I maintain a sense of responsibility to engage the family in the creation of the lives they are living. The vision board is useful to remind us of what we truly value. It makes a difference in how we see our new world and how we see each other.

What if they knew I have a purpose?

I am Clear

The older I get, the clearer I get. It has taken a long time, but I have finally figured out what I want in a man. I think the reason that I wasn't attracting Mr. Right is because I didn't know what he looked like. I don't mean how tall he is, or what color hair he has [although I do have a thing for tall, dark and handsome–then again, look where that has left me!]; what I mean is what qualities does "Mr. Right for Me" possess.

I thought I knew. It's a funny thing. When I talked to my girlfriends–all Impressive Women like me–we were all in the same boat. We were attracting men that, ultimately, didn't fit the bill. As a group one night, we all decided to go through a process that someone had learned at a seminar. We took a sheet of paper and drew a line down the middle. On the left-hand side, we began to list all of the qualities that we don't want in a man. We shared as we were going and some of them were pretty hilarious like, "chews his toenails"; others were more serious like "alcohol addiction". We laughed and cried as we all talked about our past lovers and all the things that were wrong with them. [Please note, this was not a male-bashing session. We all love men. This was a brainstorming session and we were having fun!]

Once we had a significant list drawn up that adequately and accurately listed our individual dislikes in men, it was time to get positive. Across from each of the 30-50 items [the more, the merrier, because it means you are clearer], we had to write a contrasting statement that clearly defined the characteristic we desired. In the end, some of us added things as well because we were really getting into it. Then we tore up the left side of the

185

page. We didn't want to risk putting any more energy into the negative aspects and focused only on what we truly wanted. I took my list home and continued to work on it for a couple of weeks. It is amazing how "in tune" you get to what you want when, everywhere you go, you see what you *don't* want. Brilliant! [This activity also works if you are trying to transform any other part of your life.]

Here's the amazing thing... as soon as I got clear, he showed up! I mean, he just appeared as if by magic and it seems like he has always been in my life. I have been in love with Mr. Right for Me for six months and I have never been happier. I know that I attracted him to me because of how clear I was about what would make me happy. I am so satisfied in this relationship that I don't want another one, ever. I am committed to spending the rest of my life with this guy. It may have taken me a long time to get clear, but it was the right time.

What if they knew I am clear?

I am Productive

Don't get in my way when I'm on a mission. I work at lightning speed with laser sharp focus. I will accomplish more things today than many of my colleagues will during the entire week. *What makes this Impressive Woman so productive?* It's a smart thing to ask. Imagine if everyone would tap into this... really, imagine what would get done!

The fact is that I place an extremely high value on being productive for its own sake. I value efficiency, order, and accomplishment. I enjoy the rewards that come from high sales figures and excellent customer satisfaction. I am driven to success for all the reasons that you may expect from a type A overachiever. But there is one thing that drives me to succeed more than anything else. It has become my *raison d'etre*. The motivation for my high level of productivity is *work-life balance*.

Since I became a mother, I have committed to leaving the office at the same time of day, regardless of what new sales promotion is running. It doesn't matter if it's the end of the month, quarter or fiscal calendar, I go home at 5:00 each day and I don't feel one bit guilty. If ever I was questioned or if someone [who didn't know better] thought that I was not pulling my weight, there is no shortage of evidence to back me up. Before I had children, I worked long hours. My marriage and other relationships suffered because I always put my commitment to work ahead of anything else. I felt I was obligated because it was the source of my income. I turned a corner, however, when I became pregnant and recognized the importance of cultivating relationships, especially if my husband and I were to "survive" parenthood. And we didn't want to just survive, we wanted to thrive.

With that in mind, and a growing belly, I communicated my new plan to my boss. I committed to producing the same output within fewer hours so I could be fully present with my family and friends during my down time. I would not stay late. I would not work on weekends. I would design systems and share them with my team so they understood that I was there to be productive and I would be more productive if they were on my side.

Of course, it's no surprise that the entire team jumped on the bandwagon and really embraced my philosophy. Out of ten of us, not one person works extra hours anymore and we are the top producing sales team in the district! You'd think because we are all working hard that we don't have any fun at the office, but that's not true. We are so pumped to produce every day that our energy is upbeat and positive. We celebrate our successes and support one another's goals. There are others in the office who wonder what happened and how we transformed, but they are too afraid to ask! So, *thank you* for asking. I hope you get inspired to be productive, too. It makes all the difference!

What if they knew I am productive?

I am Empowered

There is nothing in this world that comes close to the incredible sensation of *empowerment*. When you tap into this feeling, it's hard to imagine life without it. In fact, whenever you *do* step out of it—because you will—you will feel it in your body, because it knows the difference, even when you don't. Empowerment is an emotion that manifests physically, too—at least that's how I experience it

I feel taller and slimmer when I'm embracing my potential, playing the big game, fully self-expressed. My posture improves and my gait is more fluid. I think, speak and move with deliberate intent and everyone can tell. My eyes sparkle and my skin glows. I am a shining light in the darkest of rooms. My energy is infectious. I love feeling this way. Who wouldn't?

I've gotten into the habit of setting an intention to BE empowered every day. I do this in the morning, usually when I brush my teeth. [Whenever I instill a new habit, I try to connect it with something I normally do at the same time every day.] As I slowly brush my teeth, I repeat affirmations in my mind that make me feel empowered. I tell myself, *I am beautiful. I am confident. I am successful. I am competent. I am capable.* I end with a statement like, *Today I am empowered. Today, I attract abundance at every turn.* Some days, I focus on work, finances, love, friendship, or family... but really, empowerment comes in handy every day, no matter what life brings your way.

This early morning ritual is also handy when I'm stopped at traffic lights or when I'm waiting in line at Starbucks. Any time when your mind has a tendency to wander to negative thoughts, you can replace them with empowering affirmations. I have found that doing this regularly creates a habit—just like brushing your teeth—which you'll soon convert to an automatic response at those times. It's brilliant. It really works to keep you in that state of mind. And this is particularly useful if you work in a toxic environment.

I have learned to protect my energy and let go of the desire to change everyone else around me. I focus now on the one thing I can control and that is how I am being. In response to any given situation, I decide *consciously* how I will react. I have made a significant study of myself over the past few years and, when I pay close attention, I recognize patterns of response that do not serve me. Those choices usually leave me feeling disempowered, stressed out, and nervous. Now that I am exercising my heightened self-awareness, I stop myself before responding out of habit and deliberately choose a response that empowers me. What a difference it has made in my life!

Feeling good about who I am, my choices, and my life as a whole, has brought me incredible success. I am an Impressive Woman who enjoys loving relationships, a satisfying career, financial independence, and a healthy body. I am proud of the woman that I have become. It has been an incredible journey full of learning that has brought me here: stronger and happier than ever!

What if they knew I am empowered?

I am Capable

How did this happen? How did I end up in charge? Well, apparently, while I was working hard, someone took notice and decided to give me a promotion! Now I have a team of people reporting to me and a million dollar budget. Yes, it has been confirmed: I am capable!

To be honest, it's really not that big of a shock to me that this brilliant career opportunity has befallen me. Since graduating from university and starting at this company, I have been in my bliss. After studying for years, I finally had the opportunity to put what I had learned into action. There was still a lot to learn, but I have been like a sponge. I became a really good listener where, once, I was simply a good reader. I noticed that I connected more with people who had a certain learning style and then I sought to improve on that. I wanted to better understand why some teams worked more efficiently than others and why some teams were more competitive. I soaked it all up and it has served me well.

I have continued to learn from the more senior people around me. They have been incredibly supportive. I hear other friends talk about generational issues in the workplace that drive them crazy, but I haven't experienced any of that negativity. I really appreciate the knowledge that my colleagues have gained over the years. It is incredible what some of them have seen during their career. I could listen to their stories all day. They have been generous with their time, mentoring and advising me. I appreciate, too, that they all welcome my ideas at the table and never dismiss me because of my age or my gender [I was warned about that in university.] When I have a suggestion for doing things differently,

191

I am confident in my assertions; however, I have never been pushy or cocky. I respect this organization too much. I believe in the work that we are doing and I want to contribute all that I can. It wouldn't serve anyone if I was too scared or intimidated to speak up. I am an Impressive Woman, and I intend to shine!

To say that I am honoured to lead a team of experts on a project this large in scope would be an understatement. The company has shown tremendous faith in my abilities and I am humbled. I have developed a strong vision of success for the project and intend to see it through. I am surrounding myself with people whose skills complement my own. I know I will need their help. I am grateful for the trust that they are placing in me. As a team, we will succeed!

What if they knew I am capable?

I am Intelligent

I am the one that always raised her hand in class. It's funny to recall that pigtailed young girl who always had the right answer the teacher wanted. I loved to read and because school was the only place I knew that had books, I loved to go to school. I would stay late, even as early as kindergarten, to help in the library, just for the chance to be surrounded by all that knowledge. When I was particularly fortunate, the librarian would let me take an extra book (over the limit) home. She knew I'd have it finished within a few days. She understood me.

When I am in the presence of people who love to learn, I am happiest. I love my job because I work in an environment where we are tasked with solving problems of a highly delicate nature. Now I am the Impressive Woman who raises her hand all the time. While I am intelligent, I am never boastful nor complacent. I never rest on my laurels. I am continually absorbing more and more knowledge. I devour books on many different subject matters yet there never seems to be enough time to read them all.

Enter, the internet. It was like a gift from Heaven; all that information was just a click away. It was actually a bit scary for me; because of the instant access, I found myself getting addicted to my computer. Because there is always something more to learn, there was always an "excuse" for more searching. There were pros and cons to this new pastime, however, and it caused me a fair bit of angst, to be honest.

There was just so much information at my fingertips, I never knew when to stop, or which source was best. I could spend hours reading about the best way to plant a patio garden. I could research for days when finding the "best" recipe for gluten-free chocolate chip cookies. I felt compelled to read every variation and every comment. I was over-stimulated by all the intelligence. I was exhausted! I really missed the "process" of researching the "old fashioned" way. I wanted to walk to the library, chat with the employees, search the index cards, and browse through the aisles of books in search of treasure. It's really not the same when you can "google" whatever you want.

I realized that part of the excitement of learning for me has always been about the people (or at least the people in books). I really enjoy learning from people's experiences and I have found this to be lost on the internet. I have made a concerted effort to balance the research that I do with both old and new methods. I feel like I have the best of both worlds now.

In order to stay connected with my "old school" learning values, I volunteer at my neighborhood library two nights a week, compete in a weekly Scrabble league, and race through the Sunday crossword puzzle while enjoying a pot of tea. These simple pleasures keep me in touch with my joy of learning and I think this is what makes me an Impressive Woman.

What if they knew I am intelligent?

I am Dedicated

All my life I have been dedicated to helping others. I remember, as a child, walking my elderly neighbors' dog and carrying in their groceries from the car. They always gave me candy, but that's not why I did it. I remember, too, staying after school to help my teacher tidy the classroom and erase the chaulkboard. In this case, it wasn't because she needed my help; I just wanted to make a contribution because I thought she was a really great teacher.

I have always been selective, but once I choose a target, I am dedicated to distraction. Once I make a commitment to a person or an organization, then nothing will take precedence. I can be counted on despite inclement weather or bad hair days (they usually come together). I have found tremendous satisfaction in honouring this aspect of myself. It is part of being an Impressive Woman.

My connection to the elderly didn't stop once I got older. In addition to helping my neighbours with odd jobs, I began to volunteer at the local retirement home calling BINGO when I was in high school. Do you believe that I still do it once a month? I love it! It is so wonderful to be part of a program that brings joy and laughter to folks who have given so much to the community over the years. It is such a pleasure and so gratifying. I know they appreciate me, but I have to say, it truly is one of the highlights of my month.

While I no longer clean the chalk boards of my favorite teachers, my dedication to the school system didn't waver either. I have two children who are in middle school now and, as a dedicated parent, I am involved as much as possible in keeping the school a safe environment in which to learn and grow. I have organized events, volunteered in the classroom, collected recycling, and judged public speaking contests. I may not be able to give the time that some parents can, but let me assure you, that is no indication of my level of dedication to the teachers and administration at my children's school.

There is one other organization to which I have a significant commitment. Currently, I sit on the board of a community organization that mentors young entrepreneurs. Honestly, I'd really prefer to be "down in the trenches" at a tactical level because I like my contribution to be much more hands on, but I've been volunteering with this organization since I was in college and I just couldn't decline when they asked me to join the leadership team. I'm really not much for meetings and committees as I prefer to "get things done" so I managed to assign myself to the fundraising venture and plan to hit the phones every night this week and break the standing donation record. I think they will agree, in the end, that it was a good use of my time.

You see, when I put my time and effort into helping others, I want to see the benefit right away. I have never volunteered for the accolades. I have never expected anything in return. My parents taught me, at a young age, that while we are capable, we must do all that we can to help others in need. It is the neighbourly thing to do. It is the right thing to do. As an Impressive Woman, I do believe it is my responsibility to honour this part of myself; it is a bonus that I am helping others by being fully self-expressed.

What if they knew I am dedicated?

I am Sexy

There are certain days when I just don't feel all that sexy. You may know what I'm talking about. The days when you feel like hanging out in your sweatpants, eating potato chips, and watching chick flicks on the tube. But, generally, I make the effort because it really is a true expression of my essence. I am a sexy, Impressive Woman and I'm not afraid to say it (or show it)!

Today, I'm feeling it. Today, there's something in the air. I looked in the mirror this morning and thought, "What will I BE today, as I count the days to my 40th birthday?" The response, which kind of shocked me, to be honest, was, "I feel sexy." I admit that I love looking at myself, naked, in the full length mirror in the morning. Is it possible that I lose weight while I sleep or have things just not settled? In any case, I feel particularly sexy in the mornings. And, today, I was feeling smokin' hot!

I decided to go with it! Here's what I'm going to do to celebrate my sexy self today:

- Paint my nails red. Oh yeah!
- Style my hair, long and straight, with just a little pouf on top.
- Shave my legs. *(Is that TMI? Just checking to see who is reading!)*
- Select clothes that accentuate my figure with vibrant colors and fabric that feels great next to my skin.
- Dance around the house to hot, sexy, dance tunes.
- Wear lip gloss and earrings. (I do this every day AND it works!)

- Smile A LOT.
- Wear boots–skirt optional–I mean, if I'm not wearing a skirt, I will wear pants but still feel good about wearing boots. Whew!
- Spend time with my man who makes me feel super sexy.
- Linger over my food, enjoying the combination of flavours in my mouth.
- Take a warm bubble bath with candles and wine. Mmmmm.
- Play sexy, soulful music in the background.
- Exchange the flannels for something a little more, um, "comfortable".

I will go to bed feeling confident in my own skin and very, very happy. Today I celebrated every inch of myself. Imagine if we all did this every day?

What if they knew I am sexy?

I am Disciplined

I am more disciplined than anyone I know. This is not a boastful statement. It is a fact. My discipline has served me well and I believe it is the key to the success I have experienced in all areas of my life. I have a reputation as an Impressive Woman and I think that many people respect me for the results that I have achieved. I have heard them say, "How does she do it? She never gets off track."

I have been blessed to be raised in a home that was very loving and very structured. I believe I was born with an innate desire for order and that works well for me. I don't consider myself rigid in thought, nor do I believe my family are; I prefer to think of it as "living life as a process". It just makes sense to me that if you have a goal, you would design a process to achieve certain milestones within a particular period of time.

I grew up managing my life in this way. "If you want dessert, eat all your vegetables." Makes sense to me. "If you want to go to the party on Friday, you have to study after school." *Does this not seem logical?* "If you want to earn a scholarship, then your priorities must be reflective of that goal. Your achievement will directly correlate to your effort." All of these statements are ones that I heard when I was young. They still seem like practical advice to me.

When it comes to organizing my life now, I still take a top-down approach. I begin with my vision of success. This is a warm fuzzy picture of what success means to me and includes images of things that I would like to accomplish in my lifetime. From that vision, I strategize how I will achieve this success, and I map out long-term goals. Working my way through the process, I eventually end up with short-term goals that can be broken down into daily habits and milestones that can be measured. It doesn't matter if the goal is to get a promotion, earn a sum of money, fall in love, lose weight, or travel the world. I believe that through discipline, anything can be achieved.

It is not something I have learned; it comes naturally to me. I do believe, however, that it can be taught. In fact, I am often asked by others to give them tips. I understand. They see how I work and admire the results and they want in. I would like to inspire them to create a similar world; but discipline is not for the faint of heart. When you are disciplined, you have to say "No" a lot. Many people, especially Impressive Women, are uncomfortable with that. It stresses them out. A disciplined woman, however, does not experience this stress, because she is clear about the end in the mind and the process that needs to be followed to achieve her desired result. It's really that "black and white".

Discipline requires sacrifice. If you want to save money, it means not spending. If you want to lose weight, it means not eating out. If you want the raise, it means not hanging out at the water cooler. I don't think that being disciplined is difficult because I am always so committed to my goals that I don't feel what I am "sacrificing" is more valuable than what I will gain. My goals are always steeped in tremendous meaning for me and that makes my commitment stronger. I have the utmost confidence in myself that I will achieve. There is no room for doubt. That's what it is to be disciplined. It works for me.

What if they knew I am disciplined?

I am Accomplished

I have a journal in my bedside table that I have been keeping since I got married at the age of 24. Naturally, I don't have the same journal or it would be the size of the Bible. No, I have a notebook that is the 23rd of a series. I start a new one every year and the purpose of it, is to capture all of my accomplishments.

A friend suggested this when I finished university so I would have a record when anyone asked, "What did you do today?" It seemed silly and I didn't bother until after I got married and I started to wonder what I really wanted from life. *What do I want to accomplish? What will make me feel like I have achieved success?* My journal chronicles my life in achievements, great and small.

Home. I share a lovely four bedroom home with my husband and two children. I love the way it is decorated. We designed it ourselves to have a place for everything. We entertain frequently as do the kids. Our house is the one that everyone loves to visit because it feels safe, warm, and comfortable. This is our third home. It really suits us well.

Work. I am on my third career in 20 years. Each one has been rewarding in many ways. I was always careful to choose employers whose businesses I supported. I was happy to contribute my talent to their success but when the time came that I no longer felt like I was growing intellectually, I moved on to a new challenge. It has broadened my experience and enhanced my ability to innovate and drive the success of my team.

Education. I am a voracious reader. I am always learning. I worked a few years before I went back to university to complete my graduate degree. The work experience was beneficial to my learning because it made me more critical. I have an analytical mind and it must be continuously fed or I grow stagnant and slightly unhinged. I have been involved in task forces and committees, always looking to improve and progress.

Friends. My closest friends have been in my life forever. We have been committed to keeping in touch in order to honour our bond. We share everything. We support one another. We vacation together, just us girls, and also with our families. There is nothing we wouldn't do for each other.

Family. I have cultivated a wonderful relationship with my children. I am proud to say that we enjoy each other's company and spend quality time together. As they have grown, so has our relationship but we remain committed to open communication and sharing of fear, dreams, successes and failures. We love unconditionally. We are blessed.

Travel. My husband and I have been travelling together since we were 20 years old. It is our favourite way to spend our free time. Each year we plan a big trip but we also travel around our city and province on weekends throughout the year. We believe in enjoying our "own backyard" as well as experiencing different cultures. At last count, we have visited 15 countries, every major city in Canada, and all of the parks in our province.

My journal contains the story of my life thus far. It is, by no means, complete. I intend on adding many more things yet. In fact, I started another on my 40th birthday to capture all those things that I want to do before I die. I hope I have lots of time yet because that list is long and I keep adding to it every day!

What if they knew I am accomplished?

I am Influential

As an Impressive Woman of a certain age, my circle of influence is quite large. It grows every day as I come into contact with more people. Social media has served to connect me with people who don't live near me and whom I probably would have never met otherwise. I take great pride in the influence I have over others; I also take it quite seriously.

Many, many years ago, I became fully aware of how my energy has the power to affect the world. Thirty years ago that seemed like a pretty ego-driven thing to say, but with the introduction of the World Wide Web, the world *is* our playground. In the meantime, my energy most immediately affects those who live with me, those who work with me, and those who serve me as I go about my business in my local community.

How I choose to be when I wake up each day influences what thoughts run through my head. It influences what I say and how I say it, what I do and how I do it, and most significantly, the results I experience. All of this influences everyone around me. I am a ball of energy, just like everyone else. The fact that I have so much influence doesn't let *you* off the hook. You have the same influence! I urge you to use your power wisely, and deliberately, as I do, to create the life that you desire.

During every interaction you have at your favourite coffee shop, at the library, and at the gym, be mindful that you are influencing the energy field of another person. How do you want to leave them feeling after they've been in your presence? Prepare yourself ahead of important conversations at work, at home, and in public (like when you have to return faulty merchandise) and set an intention of the influence you wish to have. You can get what you want without having to make anyone wrong and without being an "energy vampire". This takes effort, but the rewards are really worth it.

In your broader world, consider how your energy affects other people who share your space at public events. How you are being at your table sends vibrations–positive or negative–out to the surrounding tables. What kind of wave of influence do you intend to create? What do you want to attract into your life?

And then there is facebook. I admit that I don't use it very much. I go online to keep tabs on my children who are in university and to share family photos with long-lost friends but that's about it. I don't update my status very often but when I do, I am mindful of its potential impact. I laugh when I read those of my "friends". I don't think they realize how quickly "poison" spreads over the internet or how profoundly their words of wisdom [we are all full of this, you know] could serve to change how people feel about themselves. It is a choice. Beware. Take heed. An Impressive Woman has a duty, in my mind, to use her considerable influence to make a positive difference in the world. Regardless of what your age, position, or background, you have that power.

What if they knew I am influential?

I am Beautiful

What makes people beautiful? It is the color of their eyes, the size of their boobs, or the way they smile? Beauty is in the eye of the beholder. I think when we see beauty, we feel beauty, and it transforms us. We spend a lot of time looking elsewhere for it, but when we truly love ourselves, we find that it was with us all along.

It took years for me to accept that I am beautiful. I was too busy finding fault with my appearance. I didn't realize that with every condemnation, I was damaging my self esteem and that was depleting my positive energy. Have you ever been in the presence of an Impressive Woman who truly loves herself? She is the most beautiful woman in the world! She shines. Her eyes sparkle. She smiles broadly. She carries herself with confidence. She makes you feel like you are the most important (and most beautiful person) in the world. Amazing! That is the effect we can have on other people when we recognize and honour the beauty we are.

I started a new bedtime ritual so I could reprogram my subconscious mind to accept fully that I am beautiful. After I remove my makeup and brush my teeth, I take a full minute to examine my face in the vanity mirror. I review all the lines–big and small–and examine the blemishes and spots. I smile at myself. I peer deeply into my eyes and I say, "You are beautiful." When I lie in bed, I spend just a few minutes recalling how I honoured my beauty that day, how I was ashamed of myself, and how each situation made me feel. I affirm to myself that I am, indeed, beautiful and that I will be proud to show my beauty to the world tomorrow.

When I began doing this, it was uncomfortable. I'm not sure if anyone ever told me I was beautiful besides men who were about to sleep with me. A part of me internalized that being beautiful was all about sex, but I have learned that it isn't true. I just had to get clear about what "beauty" meant to me. To me, a beautiful person is one who shines, who places value on herself, and who wants to make a positive difference in the world. There is beauty surrounding us every day and, because of this new ritual, I have become much more aware of it.

I smile now when I recognize beauty at the mall, at the theatre, and at my son's soccer game. I honour it and where appropriate, I will tell people that I think they are beautiful. We all need to hear it. I need to hear it. And, now I believe it.

What if they knew I am beautiful?

I am Enough

Like practically every other person on the planet, there have been times when I have felt inadequate. In fact, I think I spent my entire 20s there! But, no more! This Impressive Woman *knows* that she is good enough. I am validated not by what other people say, but by the evidence that surrounds me in my daily life.

My reflection. I get better looking every day; or rather, I fall in love with myself more each day. I admire myself in the mirror as I brush my hair and apply lip gloss. I wear clothes that feel good. I am just the right height and weight. Always.

My wallet. I own my home and car; I provide food and clothing to my family; I can afford to take a vacation every year. All of my needs are met with ease. I do not worry about money.

My contribution. The energy that I bring to my day makes a difference in the lives of others. I am a positive, enthusiastic being who is interested in continually growing and learning. I support the development of other people by serving as a mentor, coach, and guide.

My heart. I am loved by my parents, siblings, children, spouse, friends, coworkers, clients... so many people it's hard to count them all. I feel it in my core. I have a sense of security in that love that money cannot buy. It is priceless.

My pulse. That's right. I am a living, breathing human being. When I wake up every day, I thank God that I still have the privilege to be on this earth. It reminds me that God has always loved me for who I am. It brings me such peace to truly understand.

This is evidence that I have created so I no longer rely on anyone else for approval or acceptance. This has brought me joy that is infinitely sustainable. How amazing is that? I'll tell you that when I decided that I was enough, it changed my world. I felt more empowered than I had in my whole life. It couldn't touch any external validation. It didn't compare to awards, raises, promotions, greetings cards, flowers, or expensive gifts. Don't get me wrong... I still like to receive. In fact, I think it is important to demonstrate to others how much you value them by giving them tokens of affection and appreciation. I do it, too. But I don't need it anymore to know how truly valuable I am. You don't either... let it go.

What if they knew I am enough?

I am Grateful

GLORIA, 35

On Thanksgiving Day, many people throughout our great country will express thanks for family, friends, love, health, and the worldly possessions that make our existence most pleasant. These are, indeed, many of things for which I am grateful and for which I give thanks every day. Today, as I washed the dishes and listened to my children roughhousing in the basement, it came to me that I am most grateful for the freedom I have to create an empowering life.

I believe that the way in which we operate in this world is reflective of not only who we *are* but who we *choose to be* in each moment. I believe we are born into this world for a specific purpose, to learn specific things. How that manifests will be different based on the choices that we make at each turn. The potential for all women to be Impressive Women is inside of them, waiting for them to choose to be.

Because of my choices, I am here today, and very grateful for that. My past has shaped my present but the power of choice is mine to exercise. The question is: *What will I do with this power, this awesome freedom to create?* This power puts me in the driver's seat of my life. Will I set the cruise control? Will I take the turns cautiously? Will I use GPS or drive until I run out of gas? The choice is mine and it is as exhilarating as driving with the top down!

I remember the first time I went on a vacation by myself, using my power of choice to create an unforgettable trip. My mantra was that I would do "whatever I wanted, whenever I wanted with whomever I wanted". I was giddy with the expression of this freedom. It was as if I had never experienced it before. In fact, during the first few years following my divorce, I often found myself "silly" with the prospect of such control over my choices.

What I have come to understand and embrace in years since is that I have always had the freedom of choice. I just made different choices. The choices I made in the past didn't empower me. I made choices that left me feeling isolated and inferior. I finally accepted responsibility for the part I played in creating my past circumstance just like I accept the power to create a world that completely rocks! By acknowledging that we always had the power of choice and yet we chose to live in disharmony, can be humbling to say the least. It is also very healing. And we need to heal in order to step into a new world and enjoy all its glory. Why we would choose to create a present that doesn't serve us is a mystery, but it is from these choices that we can learn the greatest lessons.

Today I am thankful for family, friends, love, health, and the worldly possessions that make my existence most pleasant. I am thankful for my experiences. I am thankful for having learned this powerful lesson.

What if they knew I am grateful?

I am Blessed

I remember when I turned 40 years old, I had a really hard time coming to terms with my age. I found myself wallowing about how unfulfilling my life had been up to this point. I felt like my life would be different by the time I hit this age; I was focused on all that wasn't right in my world. One day, I was lucky enough to receive some tough love from a friend who was a couple of years older. She told me to change my perspective and start with counting my blessings. So I did.

- Children who bring me joy every time I look at them, who make me proud
- Parents who are healthy and active, who are involved in my life and my children's lives
- House that is warm, inviting, and full of good energy
- Reliable and affordable vehicle to carry me to and from work and to transport my children to their activities
- Ample food to nourish my family and keep them healthy and vital
- Friends who are dependable, loving, and fun
- Boss who never questions my work, gives me autonomy and flexibility, who trusts and values my opinion
- Co-workers who are like family, only better!
- Beautiful community with walking and hiking trails nearby
- Parks and beaches to explore

- Social network that keeps me feeling young and engaged in the community and world at large
- Financial independence which allows me to enjoy hobbies, travel, and entertainment as I wish
- Fit body that enables me to play with the children, dance with friends, and work long hours

When I read this list, it makes my life sound wonderful. If it wasn't my list, I'd think: *This person's life sounds pretty good. What is she complaining about?* I was humbled and then I snapped of it! Instead of focusing on lack, my perspective changed to one of abundance. Once I changed my mindset, my outer world also began to change. In two years, I have witnessed improvement in my health; love life; relationships with parents and children; friendship; finances; and overall mental health. While things were good before, there were places that I wanted to make improvements so I *became* part of the solution. I feel strong and capable of enjoying my life as it is in this moment and making improvements in areas where I want to expand. It's really quite simple.

I feel blessed to have had a friend who threw a bucket of cold water over me and gave me the honest truth when I needed to hear it. I was being a negative, self-centered, victim. She had known me to be an Impressive Woman but I was so stuck in my own pity party that I couldn't see myself as I truly was—as I truly am.

What if they knew I am blessed?

I am Living my Bliss

I am excited to tell you how I live. I consider myself very fortunate to have the freedom to work from home and set my own hours; it has been an amazing blessing and was integral to the deliberate creation of this Impressive Woman's incredible life. At this point, I am willing to call it a masterpiece. This is the life I envisioned when I was young. I am living in flow; I am living my bliss.

I have adopted a regimen that provides me with a foundation for success. I rise every weekday morning at 5:30AM (7:00AM on the weekend) and set my intention for the day. While I follow the same general routine each day, I allow myself the flexibility to mix it up when I'm not at optimal health or if the weather or other extraneous conditions mess with my plan. It's alright... I take it all in stride. Whatever the Universe sends my way, I receive it willingly. This attitude, adopted over the past decade of my life, has generated an incredible amount of peace in a life that was quite regularly frazzled.

My routine was developed over a number of years of trial and error, too. As with all great lessons, it didn't appear overnight and still needs tweaking from time to time as my priorities change. When setting out my plan, I consider my personal rhythms. When I rise, I need water, vitamins, and a small piece of fruit right away. I do some light stretches (I'm generally a little stiff when I wake up) and repeat several positive affirmations related to my health and vitality before setting out for a brisk walk. I prefer to exercise in the early morning, before anyone is awake. I listen to audio books while I walk. When I get home, I do some light weights to tone my upper body, and some more stretching. [Please note that I am not a fitness expert. What I choose to do is what works best for me.] While I'm working out, I play upbeat, inspirational music and sometimes dance around the room! I have a little powder room in the basement where I'll take a refreshing shower before heading upstairs to meet my family for breakfast. Before I do, I commit to a few more affirmations about the abundance of love in my life.

It is such a joy to spend dedicated time with my children and husband over a healthy meal in the morning. During the week, we don't normally see each other at lunch and about two nights a week dinners suffer interference caused by long work days and extra-curricular commitments. I have come to relish our breakfast rituals. Everyone has an assigned task that they enjoy—setting the table, making tea, dishing out fruit, and cleaning up. At this time, we all talk about our plans for the day—how we intend to "show up" and what is on our plates. If anyone needs help, that is the best time to ask. We are all present. There is nothing competing for our attention (such as electronics, friends, or work) at that time of the day.

The morning after the children go to school and my husband leaves for his office, it is so quiet in my house. The stillness is invigorating to me. I hear so much promise there. I check in with my body and my spirit to divine what I need. I have learned that what I usually need to do at that time is write. After spending time in nature, in tune with my body, and then sharing a loving space with my family, I am amply supplied to write from the heart. And that is what I will do for an hour or so. When I feel that I am done, I stop. I usually commit to a particular outcome but not how long it has to be or how much time it should take. This was another gift I received when I learned to be in flow. I allow myself to *feel* when I have written enough. Bliss!

Changing activities at regular intervals (usually 90 minutes) has proven to be very effective for me. It enhances my creativity and alertness. After writing, I generally get out of the house and run errands. The shift from *creating* to checking tasks off my list is welcomed; it taps me into my pragmatic side. I love the feeling of doing what needs to be done. It satisfies and gratifies. I celebrate with a healthy lunch and mentally prepare for my afternoon of client calls.

I have decided to work what some would call part-time hours. I don't feel like I have a "part-time" job because it is an expression of who I am as a total human being. I have chosen not to work more than 25 hours per week because this schedule provides me with the balance and harmony that I highly value. The career I have chosen, and my level of expertise, provides me with an income that is sufficient to meet my needs. I am quite happy with my choice. I work from a beautifully appointed room on the main floor of my house. I enjoy a view of the pond from the large window in my office. Connecting with nature throughout the day keeps me in a state of gratitude and joy. Helping others in my work brings me tremendous satisfaction.

I set aside time, before the family returns, to sort mail and sundry household items that need my attention. I make it a point to have everything cleared from my desk and my mind before they come home. To honour our relationships, I have committed to being completely present when I am with them. This makes me happiest.

We make dinner together, all the while, sharing the highlights of our days. We make time, too, to discuss challenges that came up. We listen; we empathize; and we provide feedback when appropriate and when asked. Ours is a home where respect is paramount. As a parent, I believe it is one of the greatest values to teach and it makes my heart full of pride to watch my children demonstrating it in their own home.

After such an incredibly fulfilling day, what could be better than curling up by the fire with my gorgeous husband and enjoying a nice cup of tea (or glass of wine)? We always carve out time for ourselves in the evenings to communicate and to show appreciation to one another. It has kept us happily together for 20 years... the foot massages and back rubs don't hurt either!

What if they knew I am living my bliss?

I am Human

To be human is to have both an Ego and a Higher Self. It is to have both Fear and Love residing within. To be human is to make mistakes and to forgive. It is to fall down and get back up. Being human is difficult and it is easy. I love being human!

I have always found the journey of this life to be quite fascinating. I consider myself a good student, too. I read and observe and participate; I try new things and explore new concepts and make up my own mind. I am confused a lot of the time but I accept that being confused is simply another of the wonders of being human.

I am particularly interested in the notion that there are only two emotions at the centre of our existence. To think that our reality is created out of fear or love seems to simplify it, doesn't it? But, does it really? And, if it does, why not accept it as simple, instead of making it more complicated? Aha! These are some of the questions that I ask myself and a few other close friends who are interested in self-inquiry like I am. As much as I enjoy the good "debate", I confess to being more experiential in the way that I learn about life. I love to read and am fascinated with theories about what motivates and excites humans, but I get really juiced about testing the truths that are espoused by philosophers and gurus.

To this end, I set out on a mission to raise my consciousness to a level where I could detach my sense of self and observe my feelings. Naturally, there are many, many, things that are happening in our bodies on a subconscious level to which I cannot connect (breathing, blinking, typing, for example) but I am trying my best here, people, so cut me a bit of slack! [I think that was my Ego talking, by the way!] My experiment required that I "check in" at prescribed intervals and record how I was feeling in that moment. I actually set the alarm on my phone to ring every 15 minutes on the first day, 30 minutes on the second, and 45 on the third. What I observed was amazing. What I learned was, indeed, enlightening.

This small experiment was just my own way of connecting with my humanness. It was not a scientifically validated assignment sanctioned by the local university or anything fancy like that. I didn't do this experiment for recognition or money. I just did it out of curiosity. I was rewarded.

I discovered that, on the whole, I am quite a positive person... or at least, when I am working on a project like this, I am in a greatly enhanced positive mental state and it may have affected my results. *Whatever.* In any case, I observed that in 80% of recorded instances, my emotions were considered positive such as caring, loving, compassionate, friendly, joyous, satisfied, fulfilled, proud, and generous. The other 20% of the time, I recorded feelings that were negative such as anxious, worried, nervous, overwhelmed, and disappointed. During the experiment, I didn't analyse anything further. The intention was to simply take note of the emotion I was feeling at the time. Interesting enough, right? Well, *inquiring minds want to know* so I set out get more insight into my humanness.

The following week, on the same three consecutive days, I recorded my feelings as I experienced them at the same intervals. My intention with this test was to determine the *root feeling* at that moment, and whether or not my higher level of consciousness would enable me to alter the emotion because I was *detached*. Interestingly [I thought], my initial numbers were little "worse" this time. But, everything happens for a reason, right? I recorded positive feelings 75% of the time. I was able to determine that, in each case, the root feeling that I was experiencing was in fact LOVE. I could feel it deep within me. It was not superficial or make believe. It was genuinely pouring out of my heart. In those moments, I could really sense that I was being ruled by my Higher Self. Likewise, I recognized clearly that the 25% of instances where I captured a negative emotion, I could feel that I was responding out of FEAR. Yes, my Ego had control. But seeing as how I am human and, therefore, have the ability to choose my responses, I was successful in almost all cases of recognizing the fear-based response and converting it by tapping into the unlimited supply of love within me. *How awesome is that???*

It really was a cool way to spend a few days but I realize that it isn't the most realistic thing for all people. Getting in touch with your feelings, however, is definitely something powerful and worth achieving. My suggestion to you, Impressive Women, is to choose a couple of times of day to deliberately check in and observe yourself. *Are you being run by your Ego or your Higher Self in that moment? How does it make you feel?* Know that you can turn the switch if you are responding out of fear. You have the power, just like I do, to manage your emotions. Don't beat yourself up if you catch yourself being negative. That would give the Ego more power! As humans, we have both these emotions for a reason. They both serve us. But love trumps fear every time! Let's fill the world with more love. There's enough to go around! Namaste.

What if they knew I am human?

I am Perfection

"She's perfect." I remember saying that when my daughter was born. It is my mission to ensure that she never forgets it. We are all born into perfection.

What do we know of fear? We only know love until we are taught fear. It is humbling to reconnect with this truth and the fact that all of humankind came from that same beautiful place. It is what connects us. It transcends religion, race, creed, gender, sexual orientation, political affiliation, and hair color. Imagine if our world was full of people who believed in the perfection of their neighbours. Imagine how perceptions would change, how communication would improve, how barriers would collapse. In the face of such love, fear cannot exist. When we see the perfection in others, we must respond with love. I would love to live in such world.

We cannot express to others what we do not feel in ourselves, however. That is why it is critical to first recognize the perfection that lies within us as individuals. My journey of self-discovery eventually led me to this realization. This awareness brightens my days and surrounds me with comfort when I think about myself as an image of perfection. All is well in the world and I feel the power of creation within me.

I choose to share this insight with you because, as an Impressive Woman, I have significant influence in my community. Whatever wisdom I have gained, I plan to share it to help ease the pain of others. It is my calling to spread light and love in the world and I feel there is much work to do. The sad fact is that many other Impressive Women struggle because they do not see the perfection within themselves. They accept the lies that they have been fed by family and society at large that they are less than perfect in every way. I may be one voice, but I am powerful in the truth, and I will spend my waking hours dedicated to the important cause of spreading this message.

What if they knew I am perfection?

I am Divine

I accept that when I live in the present moment I am connected to my true self—my divinity. In the present moment, there is no guilt about past transgressions, there is no regret; there is no worry, nor is there anxiety about what the future may hold. In the present moment, I am content to be. It is in that place, where I am conscious of the connection to my Creator and I have access to the Infinite Intelligence and Abundance that is my divine birthright.

This belief has given me the power to create a fulfilling life as an Impressive Woman. I do not question the strength within me to endure hardship, to overcome challenges, and to triumph over adversity. I have complete faith in my capacity to grow and learn from difficult lessons that life drops along my journey. When trouble comes my way, I ask myself: *What would love do?* Then I respond in turn. Fear cannot exist where love resides and that is how I fashion my life. I have control only over the way I choose to react, and I choose to react in ways that empower me and those around me. I have been a student of my life for more than four decades and I have learned that love is the answer, in all situations. Love is the right choice, always.

My morning ritual begins with a meditation. I feel a light shining through me—from to the top of my head, filling up my body, connecting me with the earth and surrounding me with love. I am protected from harm because I believe in my divinity. I ask for guidance to manage my life from the heart and experience success as I define it. I know that I am worthy of love, happiness, health, wealth, and joy. These gifts are all accessible by me when I allow myself to receive.

Regularly, throughout my day, I check in with myself to ensure I am leading with my heart and not my head. As humans, we all face similar challenges when our Ego rises and pushes fear up. I have found the practice of taking a pause every 20 minutes (the same time I need to look away from the computer screen and stretch my back), has created a habit of higher level consciousness that has served me very well.

Being mindful to respond in love has not only improved my relationships but it has improved my productivity as well. I have a clearly defined vision of success that is always top of mind, and "responding in love" really means that I honour that commitment to myself. As I do this, I facilitate the creation of the life of my dreams.

I end each day with gratitude. It is a simple practice to say, "Thank you" but it is powerful beyond measure. Counting your blessings is the key to living a blissful life. It keeps you in the present moment and connects you with the Divine, just in time to reprogram your subconscious—while you sleep. All your heart's desires will be met when you tap into the power within.

What if they knew I am divine?

I am Impressive

I have been thinking a lot about what makes me an Impressive Woman. I started to make a list—because that's what I *do*—but I was afraid I'd forget something! Whenever I set out to do anything, I strive to do my best, so I took this task seriously and felt it required deep attention and focus. [That sentence is demonstrative in itself, I believe.]

I hopped in the car and drove to my special spot where I go when I want to clear my mind from all the chatter and look for answers that come from my heart. I have a Quiet Space that overlooks the ocean, just 15 minutes from my home. I go there almost every day when the weather permits. It has a profound ability to connect me with my Higher Self. There, I fill myself with love and acceptance [as if the ocean is my supply] so I can move through life transitions with grace and confidence, and create a life that excites me. Because I lead a full life, wearing the hats of parent, daughter, entrepreneur, friend, volunteer, and lover [again, I'm worried I might be missing something], I declare this "Time at the Sea" as "Time for Me" and it has just as much importance as the other obligations in my life. I would even go so far as to suggest that it is the most important responsibility I carry: *to honour myself*.

I know what happens when I don't take time for myself. I know what it is to live on the Treadmill of Life. Years ago, I made a concerted effort to change the destructive and disempowering patterns in my world because they were not bringing me the happiness that I desired or deserved. When I began devoting time to nurture my soul and connect with a higher purpose, my life changed in more ways than I could have expected. My relationships improved from mediocre to magnificent. Parenting became a blessing, not a chore. Work became fulfilling, not mundane. I was thriving on all levels, not merely surviving. My health improved; I had more energy and vitality. I looked better. I began to take pride in my appearance because I wanted to honour myself. I let go of the need to please everyone else; I let go of my concern over the expectations of others. I stopped looking for approval because I had all the love I needed right inside myself.

I have undergone an incredible transformation in the past five years. I am pleased to report that the "work" has been worth the effort. As I move through life now with grace and confidence, I accept what is and accept the power I have to create a life that excites me. I am continually learning and growing.

I came to my Quiet Space today in search of a list of qualities that make me an Impressive Woman. I realize now, that I don't need a list. I am what I am. I love myself for the person that I have become and I am excited about all the possibilities of the future. In this moment, I am very happy and that is good enough for me.

What if they knew I am impressive?

Epilogue

I LOVE MYSELF

Since I turned 40, I have developed a deep appreciation for the Impressive Woman that I have become. When I wake each morning, I say a prayer of gratitude for all of my blessings before I even get out of bed. Then I visualize the success I will have for the day. Each day is different and brings different opportunities to make a positive impact on my world. I take this responsibility seriously and do my best each day to honour the commitment to being the best Lisa that I can be.

Just to be sure, I look in the mirror and give myself all the validation I need: *You are beautiful. You are powerful. You are capable. Thank you for being you.* When I shower, I enjoy the present moment and affirm that I am healthy and vibrant. I am grateful for the ability to contribute my talents and skills in whatever way I am guided today.

When I am challenged, I work my way through a 7-step process that I devised for my coaching clients. It has provided me peace of mind in the most difficult times.

Get Present. I come into the present moment and realize that, here, there are no problems, just my thoughts which can be changed. I allow myself the space to respond with deliberate intent instead of reacting emotionally.

Get Real. When I accept what is, I acknowledge the truth in the current situation and accept responsibility for my part in creating it. I also accept that I have the power to change certain things and it is up to me to use that power to make a difference that serves me.

Get Over It. In a place of blame and judgment, there is no room for possibility. I surrender. Knowing that everything happens for a reason, I express gratitude for the opportunity to learn and grow from every situation, good and bad. I uncover my limiting beliefs and I release them so I may heal and move on.

Get Clear. I visualize the desired outcome and allow for divine inspiration in the space that I have created by going within in search of the answers. I dream the big dream, from the heart, stretching my comfort level so I can *feel* how wonderful it is to enjoy success as I define it.

Get Engaged. I declare an unwavering commitment to honour myself with integrity because I am worthy of a life that excites me. I know what the achievement of my goals will add to my life and I accept the challenge of my dreams because I deserve to be happy.

Get Serious. I acknowledge that every choice either brings me closer to or farther away from my vision, so I back up my commitment with deliberate action that makes me proud. My confidence grows with every choice that aligns with my vision and makes subsequent choices easier until they form new habits that serve my higher purpose.

Get Support. I surround myself with a community that loves and respects me for the contribution I am in this world. I celebrate my authentic self with like-minded individuals who support my dreams and encourage my continued growth and development.

Working my way through this PROCESS [notice the acronym], leaves me in a state of pure empowerment. It helps me move through life with grace, confidence and excitement. In this space, it feels natural to send my love and light outward to everyone that comes in my path. This is the right place to be! It is a place I wish to share with as many Impressive Women (and Men) as possible. Together, we make up this wonderful world and, with a smile, the world shines brighter. I promise to do my part and appreciate the efforts of others who bring joy and happiness into my life.

I love the freedom that comes with truth. I feel comfortable saying that because I have known the bondage that comes with lies. I have known the depths of despair. I have known the pain that comes from suppressed anger. I have known the fatigue that comes from trying to please everyone and never quite being good enough. I have known the feeling of helplessness that comes when your loved one is ill. Because I have known this, I recognize the beauty in being the real me. I feel the relief that comes from healing.

I am happy. I am proud to be an Impressive Woman. I love myself.

Afterword

I Have a Voice

What I have learned through this experience has been tremendously empowering. By speaking my truth, I have relieved myself from years of tension. I have surrendered the burden of trying to please others and mask my authentic self. I have embraced every aspect of my personality. I have found the courage to accept myself as I am, as I was, and as I will be.

I am empowered when I am clear. Right now, I know who I am and what success means to me. I fully acknowledge my core values and incorporate them into my daily life as an expression of my authentic self. I am crystal clear about what I want my life to look like and I am committed to making the changes to how I am being and what I am doing so I create a life that inspires me every day.

I have a voice. I have gifts that were meant to be shared with the world. I confidently communicate to my circle of influence my commitment to create a new and wonderful life. I inspire others with my passion for living in possibility. I am building a community of people who are up for the challenge, just like I am.

Looking back over my journey thus far, I am proud as I recognize the progress I have made toward my vision of success. I feel my confidence soar every time I make a choice that is in alignment with what I truly value. I shine and people notice. They may not know what is creating the difference in how I look, but *I* know. And I smile.

In December 2011, when I was first inspired to write this book, I channelled the powerful mantra: *Stand Up, Speak Out and*

Shine. It became my mission for the upcoming year. I knew that one way I would ensure my personal success was to author this book. It has been in me for years yet I kept accumulating material! All of my experiences have brought me to this point and, for that, I am entirely grateful.

This has been a labour of love; self-love, that is. It was difficult to write many of these pages; I had to dig up a lot of memories that had been buried deep. The excavation required for Part One was downright painful. I wrote in the safety of my home, but always in solitude. It was lonely, but necessarily so. Releasing the emotions that had been suppressed for decades was not something that I wanted to do around anyone else. Writing Part Two was a welcomed shift in energy and it came at exactly the right time.

I kept my project under tight wraps and I appreciate the interest that was shown by my supporters. I thank them for their patience. I knew the time would come when I was ready to share myself with the world. That time has come and I thank you for being part of my journey.

Namaste

Conclusion

NOW THAT THEY KNOW

It is possible that there are some readers out there who feel betrayed by what I have written. You may be upset that I have told your secrets. The fact is, I hope that there are a *million* readers who believe I have told their secrets. I truly believe that this is the path to our salvation.

In order to be the greatest versions of ourselves, I believe we must first pay tribute to all the aspects that make us whole. This includes those aspects that we would like to keep out of the public eye. It is when we hide them, and pretend that they do not exist that the trouble begins. Once we create a facade, it is very difficult to undo. Along with the facade, comes the burden of having to maintain it. It is tiring. It makes us miserable.

> Cardboard masks of all the people I've been
> Thrown out, with all the rusted, tangled
> dented God Damned miseries

I have always been affected by this particular line from Jann Arden's song, "Good Mother". I finally know why. When we throw out the masks that have been hiding our authentic selves, we also let go of the pain and misery they have caused. Let's embrace the truth about who we are and release ourselves from bondage. That's sounds pretty dramatic, doesn't it? And, if you are starting to read this book here, that's an accurate assessment. I defy you to read the confessions of the Impressive Women featured in Part One and not feel their pain. These women are crying out, finally.

Thank goodness! And for those empowering affirmations in Part Two, let us all rejoice!

Now that they know... now that the secrets are out, what's next? Well, now that we are powerful and strong, standing in our truth, we can get on with the business of being Impressive Women. We can own our frailties, accept them, and live in possibility, knowing that we are beautiful, honest, and capable. We are so much stronger in our truth. We are magical. We are powerful. We are Impressive Women. And I feel truly blessed to have such great company.

Thank you for reading and sharing this book with the Impressive Women in your lives. I trust that the words that I have written will help you heal and move through your journey with grace, confidence, and excitement.

About the Author

Lisa Payne is an Impressive Woman. As a coach, speaker and author, Lisa's mission is to help women move through life transitions with grace and confidence so they can create a life that excites them. Her own journey of transformation has challenged her with chronic pain, divorce, relocation, job loss, and illness. It has also rewarded her with incredible abundance. She celebrates each day, currently living in Newfoundland & Labrador, Canada, with her two children, Joel and Sydney.